More Praise for Lite _____s and Laughter

"There is a wonderful moment when real life collides with whimsy and funny happens. That's what we have here. Lee Gaitan explores everything from napping in a recliner to being cut off in the drive-thru at McDonald's, and in each charming story, a thread of shared experience shines through. Lee keeps us chuckling to ourselves in the recognition that her world looks a lot like mine - only funnier."

–Anne Born, Publisher, The Backpack Press

"Anyone who wants to enter a world of captivating hilarity and fluent sarcasm should read this book! Epic entertainment and laughter await you!"

–Morgan Field, award-winning intuitive life coach, best-selling, award-winning author **of Epic, Sexy, You** and founder of epicsexyyou.com

"Do you let life's everyday irritations weigh you down? Let the fabulous writer and humorist, Lee Gaitan, lighten your load when you read her hilarious collection of essays, Lite Whines and Laughter. Warning: do not read while drinking fluids or with a full bladder."

–Molly Stevens, award winning writer at Shallow Reflections and author of **Boomer on the Ledge™**

"Lee Gaitan, hands down, and no I didn't say "crepey," liver spotted hands, is laugh-out-loud funny. She is doubtless the prototype for the ubiquitous LOL we all sling around carelessly as she puts into words the many stray thoughts that blast through our vacuous minds any given day. Be prepared to cry helpless tears at her funny observations and grab a pillow to stifle your laughter if you're in public."

–Jeanie Brosius King, Personal Change Specialist, co-founder of beautifulnetworkofwomen.com

"Need help navigating a world filled with lunatic drivers, robotic sales clerks, and products-a-plenty for aging skin? Look no further than Lee Gaitan's hilarious **Lite Whines and Laughter: Mild Rants and Musings on the Mundane.** From sticky buns and peeping possums to sweet nothings whispered in your good ear, **Lite Whines and Laughter** is the full tour and then some. Lee Gaitan makes the mundane magical with keen insights and humor written in a style worthy of Erma Bombeck. You need this book!"

–Mary Kay Fleming, award-winning humor essayist and Professor of Psychology, Mount St. Joseph's University

"Lite Whines and Laughter is the perfect literary snack. It goes scrumptiously well with a side order of satire, sarcasm, and wit."

–Joel Boggess, keynote speaker, bestselling author and award-winning podcaster

"I absolutely love whenever I get my hands on Lee Gaitan's latest writing. Lee has this way of describing the everyday craziness and truth of being a woman. Through her relatable stories, I find the humor in my own absurdly stressful day. I love how her tales make me not only LOL but actually ROFL with a totally unexpected SNORT at her zany, yet all too-real life."

--Ann Hoffman-Ruffner, Founder/CEO
Wayfinding Women, LLC

"Really a delightful read. Gaitan manages to take the mundane and the everyday and transform them into moments of magic and laughter."

–Award-winning poet, author and Professor of English, University of Vermont

Lite Whines and Laughter

Lee Gaitan

Cover: Design by Shoi, Shoi-Yean Mak

Published 2018 by HumorOutcasts Press
Printed in the United States of America

ISBN: 0-9994127-8-7
EAN-13: 978-0-9994127-8-7

Table of Contents

Bonus Tracks From the Vault

1.
Drive-Thru Disaster

I teach at a nearby college from 9:00 to 12:00 on weekday mornings. After class, I leave school and head off to tutor my private students. On Wednesdays I have a very short window of time to get from campus to my student's house. As a concession to my tight schedule and the need to eat and drive at the same time, I have allowed myself the once-a-week treat of a drive-thru Egg McMuffin at the McDonald's on my route. (Before the lectures start, let me assure you, my PMS days of jonesing for a monthly French fry fix are far behind me. These post-menopausal days the only other Mickey D's item I can order in good conscience is the oatmeal—which, although quite yummy and at least theoretically healthy, cannot be eaten while driving.)

Due to the antics of an out-of-control lunatic with no regard for traffic laws, human life or even (*gasp*) grammar rules, my recent midweek McMuffin deteriorated from treat to trauma. First of all, the traffic flow of the parking lot is very clearly marked as one-way. To enter the drive-thru line, one must circle the building and queue up. One MAY NOT drive up the down staircase, so to speak, and cut into the drive-thru line, heading off those customers who are rounding the building per the rule.

It was at this precise juncture that I encountered the lunatic. Just as I was about to take my rightful place as the next car in line, she came *vroooming* into the parking lot against the flow of traffic, her engine running hot enough to sear every Big Mac from here to Brazil. I tried to give her the benefit of the doubt, thinking perhaps she was fleeing the clutches of a tyrannical despot or possibly the casting director for a proposed *The Real Housewives of Hazzard County*. For her safety and that of the pedestrians in the parking lot, I waved frantically to warn her not to proceed in the wrong direction. She not only barreled on,

1

she suddenly swerved so sharply to the right I thought her left tires would lift right off the ground. With this move she effectively cut in front of me in the drive-thru lane!

Before I had a chance to react to these heinous breaches of drive-thru protocol (besides slamming on my brakes, that is), she started blaring her horn at the white minivan ahead of her and then lowered her window to shout, "Move yer ass!"

The poor woman in the minivan hung her head out the window and asked with genuine bewilderment, "Where do you want me to go? I'm in line and there are two cars ahead of me."

"Then me and him are gonna move yer ass for you!" the lunatic bellowed.

And that's when I felt compelled to act. Drive against the flow of traffic and cut me off, fine, but I will not stand for grammatically incorrect ranting! If you're going to curse someone out for absolutely no reason whatsoever, besides the fact that you are an irrational imbecile, then for crying out loud, get your subject and object pronouns straight! How far have ranting standards fallen these days anyway?

As I hit the "down" button on my window, the nut job, without warning, pulled her car out of the line and gunned it onto the highway. The lady in the minivan and I just exchanged shoulder shrugs and head shakes.

Although the unexpectedly abrupt ending to this episode felt a little anticlimactic, it was probably better that my grammar showdown never materialized. If Mayor McCheese had come out to referee under the scorching midday sun, he surely would have suffered a messy meltdown. And then the peoplein the drive-thru lane would have been blaring their horns at me—*not at I*—for delaying their orders while I dutifully scraped up His

Honor's sticky buns from the hot pavement. Next Wednesday, I'm packing my lunch!

2.
Thanks for Nothing

Okay, okay, it's not as if I can't spout the party line about how it's more blessed to give than to receive, but let's be honest, when you give, you don't really feel all that blessed until the recipient acknowledges your thoughtfulness. And it wouldn't hurt if they threw in a little something about how you look as if you'd lost weight, too. After all, they're getting the hard goods; the least they could do is throw some cheap praise your way.

I am such a compulsive thanker that I actually send thank-you cards to people for sending me a thank-you card. I sometimes worry that I will get caught in a thanking loop with someone like me and neither of us will be able to stop. We'll just go on endlessly thanking each other, sounding like the Goofy Gophers Mac and Tosh: "Thank you, my dear." "Oh, no, thank *you,* my dear." "No, no, I insist, thank *you,*" *ad infinitum.*

If my recent experiences with gift recipients are any indication, however, I needn't lose sleep worrying that I will be swept away by a giant wave of gratitude any time soon. It's been five weeks since I mailed out two separate gifts and I have yet to hear one word, grateful or otherwise, from either recipient. No card or call, not even an email or a stinking Facebook message. And bear in mind, I was hardly required to "gift" anything to either of these people—there were significantly more than six degrees of separation between us, a friends-of-friends kind of thing—but I thought it would be a nice gesture and, yes, I had been looking forward to the feeling of satisfaction that comes from knowing your efforts were appreciated.

Unable to fully believe that people could be so blatantly rude and ill-mannered as to neglect acknowledging my gift, I considered all the alternate explanations for their lack of response. Perhaps the thank-you cards were delivered to the wrong address, to a band of hooligans who shamelessly trash wrongly delivered mail rather than redirect it to the proper destination. Or maybe they were stolen out of my mailbox by someone even more desperate for recognition than I am. Or maybe they were lost in the mail altogether, even though every instance I know of where something was "lost" in the mail it was "lost" only by virtue of never having been put in the mail in the first place. This is particularly true with alimony checks. Still, it remains a possibility, and if I accept that it's possible that the cards got lost in the mail, then I must concede that it's equally possible that the gifts themselves got lost and never reached their intended destinations. So, I will reserve final judgment on the two mailed-gift recipients until I figure out a way to confirm that they in fact received the packages. (I will ply our common friend with heart-healthy chocolate until she agrees to grill the offenders on my behalf.)

Unfortunately, there can be no such reprieve from judgment for a third recipient, as I delivered the gift to her in person, thus eliminating all doubt about whether or not she had received it. And I must say her reaction, or more precisely her complete lack thereof, was the most stunningly rude of all. I presented her with the gift bag before work one morning last week. She took the bag from my hand, pushed it to a corner of her desk and nonchalantly remarked, "Oh, I have a gift bag with this same design." And that was it. I stood there for a moment and then awkwardly babbled something about just wanting to give her a little something for the baby she'd had shortly before she started working in my office (which, P.S., was before I even knew her). She moved the tissue aside a little, peered in the bag and then pushed it aside again to continue typing.

Feeling more uncomfortable by the second, I excused myself with, "Well, okay, that's all then, um, thanks" and scurried out of her office. When I got back to my desk, I realized that I had actually thanked her! For what? For letting me give her a present for which she offered no thanks? Oh, well, at least someone got thanked, I thought. Mac and Tosh would be proud.

But next time I thank someone for letting me give them a present, I suppose I should add something about how much thinner they look. After all, it's the polite thing to do.

3.
Gee, You Shouldn't Have. . .Really

I think I speak for most women when I say I love to get presents. Birthdays, anniversaries, St. Swithin's Day—all occasions that demand presents, in my opinion. I love getting presents so much that I devised a plan to rotate among different religions throughout the year in order to increase my gift-getting opportunities. (And in the process I learned that three separate holidays intersect on February 2—the Druid Imbolc, the Christian Candlemas and the secular Ground Hog Day. Store that little nugget away for your next trivia night.)

It's important to note that I am the ideal gift recipient. I don't require expensive purchases and I am extremely easy to please. From aardvark-shaped candles to dry erase markers, I think everything is a treat. Once I even graciously accepted a pair of patterned XXL pantyhose from a student—and gave growing into them a real shot when another student gave me a gift card to Ben & Jerry's.

But recently I have run up against a gift-getting situation that I'm not sure how to handle. On three separate occasions, from three separate and unrelated people, I have received various anti-wrinkle potions formulated for "aging skin." I'm not talking about fancy body lotion sets that are more cosmetic than therapeutic. I'm talking about down-and-dirty, pull-no-punches wrinkle cream for industrial strength Shar-Pei faces. And each person that "gifted" me implied pretty much the same thing, saying, "I saw this and thought of you" or "I wanted to get you something you could really use." Seriously? Did no one but me get the memo that 70 is the new thirteen and a half? (With this new math, I'm practically an embryo.)

I can't decide whether to be grateful or insulted. On the one (crepe-y) hand, these are expensive products, ones I really did want to try sometime, but on the other (liver-spotted) hand, shouldn't I be the one to determine when that time has come? I was silently contemplating this very question when my husband walked in the room.

"Hey, what are you doing just sitting around?" he asked. "Lesser Quinquatrus starts tomorrow, doesn't it? I figured you'd have the whole house decorated by now."

He was right. It was the eve of Lesser Quinquatrus, the ancient Roman holiday celebrating flute players (which I actually was in my youth), but I wasn't feeling particularly festive. "I've decided to cut back on holidays for a while," I said with a shrug.

"But what about your big plan to increase your gift-getting opportunities?" he asked, somewhat shocked.

"I'm putting that on hold for now," I replied. "Let's just say it developed a wrinkle or two I hadn't foreseen and leave it at that."

You know what, folks, here's a little tip—next St. Swithin's Day, just say it with cash!

4.
Can You Hear Me Now?

According to a short Google search I just conducted, the best historic evidence suggests that marriage as a formal institution has existed for nearly 5,000 years. In all that time, there has likely never been one single wife who, at some point or other, didn't blurt out these words of frustration to her husband: "You don't listen to me!"

I'd even bet that if we dialed the clock all the way back to prehistoric times when relationships were less formally defined, we'd hear some exasperated cavewoman crying out, "Ug, ug, ugggggggggg!" at a caveman who had no clue why she was frustrated enough with him to club *herself* on the head.

Communication challenges between my Colombian husband and me go beyond his having a "Y" chromosome. For one thing, English is not his first language, and Spanish is not mine. This led to some cross-cultural misunderstandings in the beginning of our relationship wherein he wondered why I was asking him to close the "chicken" (kitchen) door and I wondered why he mentioned his "tonsils" so frequently. (He was actually saying *entonces,* which means "then" in Spanish).

And for another thing, he has a 40% hearing loss in his left ear from repeatedly rupturing his eardrum while diving in his younger days. Whenever I'm feeling kind of frisky, I have to be sure to whisper sweet nothings in his *good* ear or there's not going to be much action.

Neither second language struggles nor, especially, hearing loss should be treated lightly, but we try to see the humor in the situation. My husband must wear earplugs whenever he swims to prevent contracting an ear infection, which could further compromise his hearing. When he forgot to take them along on our honeymoon ten years ago, he still insisted, despite my repeated bilingual warnings, on jumping in the South Beach surf every day and swimming halfway to Spain. By week's end, as I predicted, he had a raging infection and couldn't hear anything out of the affected ear. When we got home, he went straight to the ENT.

"Doctor, it's a very bad situation for me," he explained with some desperation. "I just got married last week and I can't hear anything my wife says with my left ear."

"Oh, no, that's not a good way to start a marriage," she replied sympathetically.

"It certainly isn't," he continued, "because I can still hear her very clearly with the right one."

Ha, ha, he's such a funny man. But a few weeks ago, I stopped laughing. He seemed to be paying even less attention to what I said than usual, and I had a sinking feeling he was going completely deaf. I urged him to schedule an appointment with the audiologist for a retest, and I waited anxiously the day of his appointment to find out the results. As soon as I got home from work, I pounced on him, unable to wait a second more to learn if he was losing his hearing.

"Well?" I intoned, my voice tense.

"Well," he started, "there's good news and some not really bad, but interesting news."

"What are you talking about?" I asked impatiently. "Just tell me!"

He unfolded a paper with the test results and laid it on the counter. He said he knew I wouldn't believe his account unless I saw the actual report from the audiologist.

"Why would I doubt you?" I asked, confused.

"Just read it," he said.

The report showed that while he hadn't exactly lost hearing overall, his ability to hear sounds within a specific frequency range was fairly impaired. The precise range was the one within which *90% of all female voices* fall. He could hear above or below that range just fine. It took a moment for me to process the implications of this new information.

"So," I said, enunciating clearly into his good ear, "you are telling me that you are nearly physically incapable of listening to me," I said.

"That's correct," he said.

"That you're more likely to respond to one of those 'silent' dog whistles than to the sound of my voice," I continued.

"Also correct," he replied.

"And that you could hear, say, Barry White—*grumbling from the great beyond*—but not me, standing in front of you in the here and now."

"Correct again," he said.

How convenient, I thought. My husband had the perfect "out" most other men only dream of, an excuse for everything from not taking out the garbage to not making the dinner reservations. If this information ever fell into the wrong hands, every married man on the planet would take up diving, intent on destroying his hearing capacity in the "wife frequency range." They'd likely consider it a small sacrifice for living a nag-free life.

So, ladies, consider this a cautionary tale in the interest of preserving marital bliss. Do everything you can to keep your husband in the shallow end of the pool. And should he slip away and plunge off the high dive, remember that you still have a secret weapon to get his attention, the dog whistle. Don't be afraid to use it. And you know how to whistle, don't you? You just put your lips together and blow. It certainly did the trick for Lauren Bacall and Humphrey Bogart!

5.
Lost in Translation

If you've ever been offered baked goods made "from scratching" or asked if you give hard "testes," there's a good chance you teach English as a Second Language (ESL). Our crazy language is a minefield of unintended consequences, just waiting to ambush new learners. One seemingly insignificant change in spelling or pronunciation can affect meaning in a very significant way. I had the same experience a few years ago when I changed one teensy little vowel in Italian and instead of asking for my room key ended up inviting a hotel clerk in Florence to have sex with me. In the most explicit terms possible. (Not that I was opposed to the idea, mind you, but I still needed my key.)

Those teensy little changes will get you every time. That's all it took for one of my favorite students to become temporarily— but hilariously—lost in translation. Olga had been in the U.S. only a few weeks when she enrolled in my adult ESL class. One day she came to my room about fifteen minutes early and we began chatting. She told me how hard she was working outside of class to improve her English. She had started reading the newspaper in English, she said, and as a result, she'd made an important life decision.

"I read an article about how is good for the woman to have the condom," she told me with great certainty. "So, I decide I want buy the condom."

As Diet Coke was shooting out of my nose, she quickly reassured me of the wisdom of her plan.

"*Si, si*, Lee, I think is very good idea," she insisted, nodding her head vigorously. "You have the condom, Lee?" she asked.

"Well, not on me," I said, a little flustered. "I don't really, I mean, my husband had a vas—um, never mind. No, I don't have a condom."

She was looking at me quizzically when suddenly—*pop*—the light bulb flipped on for her, but not quite all the way. "Oh, Lee, I know what you think. You think I am crazy. Is so much money for buy the condom."

"No, it's not that," I said, puzzled.

"No worry, Lee," she continued. "Is cheap for me because I no buy new condom. I only buy used!" She dramatically drew out the word "used" for about three syllables.

I couldn't even speak. All I could picture was a clothesline of freshly laundered condoms, just a-swinging in the breeze.

In my head I was screaming, *Oh, dear God, here's ten bucks— please splurge, buy new!*

Then suddenly—*pop*—the light bulb again flipped on, but this time for me and, I was pretty sure, all the way. "Olga, what do you think a condom is?" I asked.

"Uh, is like apartment," she answered with a casual shrug of her shoulders.

"No, my dear Olga, it is most certainly not like an apartment," I said emphatically.

I then filled her in on the difference between "condo" and "condom." One teensy little letter.

I don't believe I've ever seen the particular shade of red her face turned. When the blood, shock and laughter finally receded, she shook her head and said, "Ah, *si,* it is like you say in the class. One little letter makes the big difference."

Ah, *si*, indeed it does. And in this case, adding one teensy little "m" could be the difference between converting that spare bedroom in your condo into a home office…or a nursery.

6.
Fork This

"Birds do it, bees do it, even educated fleas do it." It seems, in fact, that absolutely everyone can do it. Everyone except me, that is. I am, of course, talking about eating with chopsticks. Here I am, a decent representative of the species homo sapiens, occupying the highest rung on the evolutionary ladder, yet I have apparently not developed the manual dexterity of an educated flea. Likely not even that of an uneducated one. How is this possible?

How can my fingers, which perform so competently in many other situations, fail me so thoroughly when I try to manipulate two simple slivers of wood? I stare at my fingers and they look so normal, so functional. And, indeed, they do function quite nicely in many other ways. They have yet to meet the pimple they couldn't pick or the mosquito bite they couldn't scratch to the point of infection. They point, snap and twiddle with grace and ease, with true mastery, I daresay. And their ability to silently and efficiently communicate a message is unmatched. Each finger moves in perfect coordination to signal everything from "OK" to "bye-bye." (And sometimes, on a really bad day, one finger has acted alone to communicate my feelings quite accurately.) Yet, deposit a pair of chopsticks in my grip and suddenly all that expertise goes out the window. I might as well be wearing boxing mitts for all the grace and coordination my fingers display.

Why can't I do this? I have watched everyone from toddlers to centenarians effortlessly move all manner of victuals, from a single grain of rice to an oversized dumpling, from plate to mouth, with nary a slip or a drip. Not fair! Everyone in my family, the American *and* Italian *and* Colombian sides, can handle a pair of chopsticks with no more effort than it takes to pick up a pencil and jot down a phone number. I have even witnessed my former internist, a man famous for having fingers like five fat sausages, wielding a pair at Panda Express with pinpoint precision. Those sausage hands could barely *pick up* a scalpel, much less perform surgery with one, yet somehow magic happens with the chopsticks.

Awhile back I decided to give the chopsticks one more try, in preparation for my lunch with a group of my adult ESL students from Korea, Japan and Taiwan. Talk about performance anxiety. I didn't want to look like the stupid American and embarrass them at the restaurant, so I practiced every day for a week. I even got my neighbor from Thailand to tutor me.

Finally, luncheon day arrived and I swear to you, I tried. I really, really tried. First, the chopsticks fell completely out of my hand. Then they crossed like scissors, sending a bean, a cashew and a glob of brown sauce shooting across the table. Exasperated, humiliated and really hungry, I was about to put one stick in my fist and stab my food with it when one of my ever-gracious students leaned in and gently asked, "Miss Lee, would you like a fork?"

"Yes, oh, yes," I replied, grateful and relieved. "I think that might be best for all concerned." I savored every remaining bite of that exquisite meal.

I have decided to accept that I am hopelessly chopstick-impaired. And if my friends or family try to shame me about it, as has happened in the past, I will simply pick up a piece of tined flatware and ever so politely tell them to "fork off!"

7.
Click to Bypass the Personal Touch

In our often cold and impersonal modern world, you would think a business that boasts of delivering its services with "a personal touch" would be something to celebrate.

Yes, you would think that. And you would be dead wrong in this instance. Believe it or not, the personal touch can really screw things up. The week before Mother's Day I started scouring the worldwide web for an appropriate mother-to-be present for my daughter. The choices ran the gamut from a $4,000 bracelet with the word "Baby" spelled out in diamonds to an $8.99 t-shirt with an airbrushed "Baby" above a big arrow pointing south. Neither of those seemed a good fit—the former for my wallet, the latter for my sense of decorum.

I was about to give up when I came across a tasteful, moderately priced "milestone" necklace, a jewelry term I'd actually never heard of until that very moment, perhaps because most of the milestones I've reached haven't quite warranted jewelry. (Do they make Pandora charms for "first gray eyebrow hair" or "impressive back fat"?)

The milestone necklace consisted of a sterling silver chain and bar pendant, set with a single birthstone. "Minimalist style meets the unique personality and beauty of birthstones" read the description. Perfect, I thought, and I clicked to select the chain and one pendant with an October birthstone. And that's when the personal touch overkill began. Every time I clicked "add to cart," a pop-up "click to personalize" button prevented me from adding the necklace to my cart. I didn't want to personalize the pendant because the baby has not been born yet and she doesn't have a name. I was already taking a chance on the October birthstone because back in 1982, the mamma of this baby was supposed to come in March and she waited until April 7th to make her debut.

After several unsuccessful attempts to "proceed to check-out," I called the customer service number, whereupon I was directed to read this line in the product description:
Each pendant can be engraved with a name or message, up to ten characters on each side.

Me: Yes, that's a lovely idea, but I don't actually want to personalize it now.

Rep: Ma'am, the personalizing is free.

Me: Yes, that's wonderful, but the baby hasn't been born and I have no idea what the name will be. I just want to buy the necklace without adding a name.

Rep: You don't want to personalize it?

Me: Correct, I don't want to personalize it.

Rep: Do you understand you cannot buy it now and send it back later to have it personalized?

Me: Oh, yes, of course. After the baby is born, I'll have the necklace engraved somewhere.

Rep: But if you personalize it now, it is free. Do you understand we do not charge extra for personalizing the necklace?

Me: Yes, but do you understand that I don't know what the baby's name is? (*Trying to keep my sense of humor*) Hey, if I choose a name and put it on the necklace, will the parents be obligated to call the baby that after she's born?

Rep: (*Dead serious and redirecting my attention back to "the line."*) Ma'am, it clearly states in the description that each pendant can be engraved with a name or message, up to ten characters on each side. Do you understand what that means?

Me: Yes, it means *can* be engraved, not *must* be engraved. Can is ability, must is requirement. (*Was I really going to have to teach a grammar lesson on modals to get this damned necklace?*)

Rep: If you don't want to personalize it, then we cannot sell you this piece.

Me: Are you kidding me? I just want the necklace, plain, nothing engraved on it. That's even less work for your people, so why can't I buy it?

Rep: We only sell personalized items. That's why there is a "personalize" button on our website.

Me: Surely you can bypass that option on your end?

Rep: (*Aghast*) Oh, no, ma'am! It's not possible to bypass the system. The system is the system. And the description clearly states items can be engraved.

Me: (*My head in my hands*) Again with the "can." Oh, dear God, our civilization is doomed. Good-bye.

Further calls to supervisors and managers yielded the same result. I was about to grab an ice pick to jam into my eye when I decided to search the interwebs one more time instead. Lo and behold, I found the exact same necklace for a little higher price on another site. And, I was able to decline the personalizing option on this site! Oh, happy day, I thought...until I realized that declining to personalize added almost $100 to the total!

With the death knell of intelligent life tolling loudly in the background, I returned to the original website, clicked "personalize" and entered my message. I toyed with typing in "Welcome to this insane, screwed-up world where idiots who don't know what modals are or what they mean are allowed access to technology and software programs that they cannot properly manage. Get used to it, kid. Love, Nonna."

But that seemed like a rather harsh greeting for not only a newborn, but my first grandchild to boot. Besides, it was way over the ten-character limit. So I settled for a lame "Baby Girl" and explained to my daughter that I would replace the pendant with a *personalized* one after the baby arrived.

In the meantime, I can think of a personalized message or two for those customer service people, but since I'm about to be a grandmother, perhaps I'd better tone it down a little. I'll just leave it at a simple "Kiss my modal!" and bypass what I'm really thinking!

8.
Love with a Perfect Stranger (and we met online!)

The winter of 2014 was an exceedingly hard one for me. My mother passed away and I faced a significant health scare of my own. The call I received giving me the all clear on my follow-up tests was the first good news I'd had in weeks, and I let out a sigh of relief strong enough to rustle the spring buds on the trees outside my window. Maybe it was the giddiness of gratitude over my test results or maybe the low-grade spring fever I was running, but what happened next was completely out of character for me. I hung up the phone and for the first time in my life, I went looking for love online. Looking for, as the kids say, a hook-up. With a total stranger.

Fingers trembling, I began Googling sites, nervous and embarrassed even though I was alone. I was scrolling through photo after photo of prospects, none of which caught my eye, when suddenly, there he was, staring out from the computer screen. Strawberry blond hair, flecked with gold, and light brown eyes that seemed to penetrate me. I was certain he was the one. Was it because he reminded me of a past love? Maybe, I don't know. All I knew at that moment was I wanted him and I wanted him *bad*.

My heart was racing as I wondered if I could I really go through with it. Could I seriously bring a third party into our home to spice things up for my husband and me? To be honest, it had been a secret fantasy for a while. I hadn't broached the subject with my husband, but I often sensed that he, too, felt something was missing in our relationship, an element of excitement that we'd lost along the way. We'd grown a bit too comfortable and predictable with each other. Maybe Mr. Brown Eyes was just what we needed to heat things up.

When my husband came home, I told him what I'd done. Initially reluctant, he finally agreed to meet Mr. Brown Eyes the following Saturday in a public place. I was delirious with delight.

"Let's not get ahead of ourselves," he said evenly. "Let's just see how this goes. You and I both have to feel comfortable with him."

I spotted him among the crowd the minute my husband and I walked through the door that fateful Saturday morning. He was even better looking in person than in his photo, his reddish gold hair brilliantly shining in the morning sunlight that streamed through the window.

"Harper?" I asked rhetorically as I sidled up next to him.

He swung his head in my direction, his caramel eyes meeting my gaze as he politely offered to shake my hand. When I heard him speak, I knew I was done for. And my husband wasn't far behind. This guy had us at "Woof."

From that moment on, there was little doubt that Harper was the third party we were looking for. He was a handsome boy with a sturdy build and a demeanor so dignified he practically barked with a British accent. In fact, if we had any reservation at all, it was that he seemed almost a little too reserved. I loved that he walked so nicely on his leash and sat calmly while my husband and I made all the adoption arrangements, but I was a little concerned that he might not be playful.

I needn't have lost any sleep over the playfulness issue. Since my husband and I were going to be traveling the next few days, we arranged for the adoption coordinator to bring Harper to our house the following week. The dog that burst through our front door the next Saturday certainly looked like Harper, but he bore no resemblance in manner to the dog we'd met a week before. He was an explosive mix of nonstop jumping, spinning and rolling. He tore around the house at top speed, sending throw rugs sailing through the air like magic carpets and leaving a cloud of dust and dog hair in his wake. Every last vestige of reserve was gone and there was no doubt that he was barking in full-out, top-volume American!

My husband and I stared at each other in complete shock, only half joking when we wondered aloud if doggie Quaaludes had been involved the week before. Who knew, but one thing was certain—this was not the dog we had signed on the dotted line for, not the one we had agreed to take into our home and love forever. No, this was not that dog! This was a dog even more wonderful than we had realized the week before! We'd gone looking for someone to spice things up and now we had him—cayenne, curry and chili pepper rolled into one. Harper was the exact ingredient our lives had been missing. For the first time since our last dog, our wonderful "Jif the Exuberant," had crossed the rainbow bridge, our home and our hearts felt complete.

It's been two years since we bade farewell to order and tidiness and gratefully welcomed chaos and calamity back into our lives. We are awakened each morning with the poke of a wet nose instead of the buzz of an alarm clock and our time is measured in ear scratches and belly rubs, not minutes and hours. And we couldn't be happier. Our third party, our online love, our wild, crazy and sweet, sweet, sweet Harper boy is truly the spice of our lives.

9.
The Eyes Have It

Okay, Bobbi Brown, now I'm mad! You, the savior who came to my rescue after Lancôme cavalierly turned their backs on me a few years ago, have just managed to tick me off. Make no mistake, I am a woman who needs your eyeliner—not likes or enjoys, but needs, as in requires for my daily survival.

In an unfair twist of fate, I ended up with a completely mismatched set of features: dark brown hair, bestowed first by nature and in the last decade or so by L'Oreal, incongruously coupled with very fair skin, light eyes and nearly invisible lashes. I'm not kidding, my lashes, although of decent length, are practically clear. It seems to violate some natural law for a person to have such dark hairs springing from her head yet such colorless ones rimming her eyes, but that's what I have.

If I am not wearing eye make-up, my eyes recede into nothingness, blending in so completely with my complexion that it looks as if I have pinholes instead of eyes. And with increasing age has come the increasing transparency of my eyelids, so that they now have a pinkish, inflamed hue to them, not unlike those of a white rat.

So, yes, eyeliner is essential for me if I want to avoid shrieks of "Run, it's the rat lady" as small children flee from me in horror. In fact, I have found that for everyday wear, I can actually skip the mascara and shadow as long as I use a good eyeliner, a move that simultaneously safeguards the emotional well-being of impressionable children and affords me an extra snooze cycle on workday mornings.

Until about four years ago, my go-to product was Lancôme's cake eyeliner applied with a wet brush, but as has happened with so many of my beloved products over the years—not to mention my first husband— it up and dumped me without any warning. When I found out Lancôme's liner was being discontinued, I bought up all the remaining stock I could, but eventually I came to the end of my stash. I frantically scoured cosmetics counters and the internet for a comparable replacement, to no avail. The eyeliner market was heavily flooded with various types of pencils and pens, but none of them were suited to my eyelid specifications. The pencils were too smeary and the pens were too hard to control. And neither was compatible with upper lid "crepey-ness"

I was completely bereft...until, like manna from heaven, Bobbi Brown Long-Wear Gel Eyeliner fell into my hands, via my friend in St. Louis, who picked it up on QVC, and my daughter, who bought it at a mall in Providence, Rhode Island—both in the same week, so it was obviously fate. This liner, in Espresso Ink, is a magnificent product, no hyperbole at all here. It slides, glides, and hides. It defines without smearing, peeling or cracking. It just about restored my will to live when I used it for the first time, and I have lined my eyelids in Espresso Ink nearly every day since. At twenty-three bucks a pop, it's not exactly bargain priced, but you can't put a price on magnificence.

So what's the problem, you ask. You know the saying about having too much of a good thing? Well, that is the problem in a nutshell, or a .1-ounce/3 gram glass jar, in this case. Although that sounds like a miniscule amount, it is actually a lot of eyeliner. So much liner, in fact, that it is virtually impossible to get to the bottom of the jar before its "gel-iness" expires. Short of using it to draw a mustache, beard and sideburns every day, there is no way one woman with the standard issue of two upper and two lower lids can go through that much liner before its luxuriously smooth texture turns to dehydrated brittle clumps.

Every time I reach this point, it's the same routine. Unable to bring myself to throw out half a jar—that's $11.50 worth—of liner, I try different ways to extend its usability. This morning I excavated the top crusted layers with a cuticle pusher, trying to uncover a little pocket of still pliable gel; I applied the clumps one at a time and tried to fuse them together to form a line; I wet the brush with water and even a bit of moisturizer. All epic fails, as the kids say.

I finally acknowledged defeat, threw out the jar and headed off to Nordstrom to shell out another $23.00, plus tax, for a jar of gel liner, knowing full well that half of it will be lost to me. What is the reasoning here, Bobbi? Why not sell half as much for half the price and eliminate not only the waste, but also my frustration. I appreciate a manufacturer who actually tries to give you more than you expected, but if half of the product goes bad before you have enough time to use it, what's the point? I can't live without you, Bobbi, but I gotta be honest here, a little of you goes a long way!

10.
Hair Peace

As the rock group Three Dog Night crooned back in the '70s, I have never been to Spain – or Portugal, for that matter. My hair, however, is fast approaching the size of the Iberian Peninsula. In fact, I've started referring to my neck as my isthmus. A stubborn, moisture-laden weather pattern has had my hair in its oppressive grip for the past 25 days. With humidity levels in the 700% range, my hair grows big, bigger and more bigger by the nanosecond. Let me tell you, *this* is the greenhouse effect that I'd like to see some experts tackle, one they could really sink their combs' teeth into (although they'd likely never see their combs again as my Iberian Peninsula hair doubles as the Bermuda Triangle). It's nothing for small objects, such as barrettes, headbands and parakeets, to stay lost in my hair for days, weeks, even years. I'm pretty sure the bobby pin that shook loose from my hair the other day was part of the anchoring system for a French twist installed for my junior prom.

If you think I'm exaggerating or imagining things, you have never lived with my hair. Did I imagine the round brush that had to be cut free after becoming hopelessly tangled in my tresses? No. Did I imagine the barrette—bulging with the girth of my plumped-up locks—that finally gave way and *boinged* off my head, nearly putting out the eye of an innocent bystander? I did not. And finally, did I imagine the stage-whispered choruses of "Ch-ch-ch-chia" that followed me everywhere I went one particularly muggy day last summer? I assure you I did not.

Taming my hair is a formidable task even when the isobars are arranged in a more favorable pattern. Understand that we are talking about hair whose routine care and maintenance involves the use of a self-propelled Lawnboy and a weed whacker. Hair that regularly qualifies as the "two" in "two-for-one" memberships. But I have to be careful what I say here because my hair is like a horse; it smells fear. If it catches even a whiff of uncertainty—much less outright fear—coming from me, I might as well invest in a hat factory because, hair-wise, I've lost the upper hand. Better to regard my hair as a spoiled pet who has been overindulged to the point of getting inflated ideas that far exceed his station in life. Better to keep a firm hand—or two—on it at all times. In other words, I must show my hair who's boss.

And I have assembled an arsenal of hair weaponry to help me do just that. From texturizers to contouring lotions to anti-frizz creams, I'm armed and ready for battle. I've been more or less holding my own during this recent soggy siege, but there have been days when I've been forced to take more drastic measures against my expanding hair—like actually hosing it down so it didn't block my sightline to the rearview mirror. (It's possible I'm now developing root rot.) But since the latest weather report holds no promise of swift relief, I had better try to make the best of the situation. You know, look for the positive in having hair the size of two countries. Use this as an opportunity to learn more about the cultures of Spain and Portugal. Hey, I could even dust off that old pair of castanets my sister brought back from Madrid years ago. There's just one problem…I have to untangle them from the back of my head first.

11.
I Forgot to Remember

Man, I really hate when I forget to do things. I don't mean forget-to-go-to-the-dry-cleaners kinds of things, which I do on a regular basis, or even forget-to-put-your-dentures-in-before-going-to-work kinds of things, which I only do on a semi-regular basis. I mean things like "be independently wealthy" or "become the ruler of several small nation states" or "lose 15 pounds." I had fully intended to do these things—heck, they were numbers 1-3 on my list, for crying out loud—and then, somehow, I just *forgot*. And am I ever steamed now that I have started remembering all the things I have forgotten to do. For example, it completely slipped my mind that my husband and I were going to the beach early next month and, consequently, I forgot to lose weight. (I did, however, remember to eat a giant bag of peanut M&Ms, so now I have to remember to pack my collection of tasteful muumuu ensembles for day and evening wear.)

It's the same situation with the independently wealthy thing. Somehow I simply *forgot* to do it. This morning as I was struggling to stretch my double-digit checking account balance to cover a triple-digit credit card bill, I had a sudden "aha" moment wherein I exclaimed aloud, "Oh, shoot, I forgot to be filthy rich!" How could that have happened, I wondered? Had I, at some point in the past—a time I no longer recall, of course— rejected being filthy rich as a worthy goal? Had I, at some earlier time, also determined that being the ruler of several small nation states had too big a downside for me? I was pondering these questions quite seriously when I saw this quotation posted on my friend's Facebook page that seemed to explain it all: *I was going to conquer the world...but then I saw something shiny.*

Wow, what a revelation! This explains everything, I thought. Never had I consciously rejected any of my original goals in favor of others. Never had I deemed them unworthy pursuits and redirected my course. I had simply gotten distracted. Why, several times I'd been on my way to filthy richness or even zip-my-jeans thinness and then I'd started picking at my acrylic nails or sometimes the pills on my sweater and lost my train of thought. Often for years at a time!

Oh, yes, I see it all so clearly, and now that I do, I am determined not to be distracted anymore. From here on out, it's full speed ahead with to-do list items 1, 2 and—oh, my gosh, look, a rainbow! I love rainbows, such pretty colors, purple is my favorite color, I have a purple umbrella in my car, I need to wash my car . . . wait, was I saying something before about "full-speed ahead"? Yeah, I think I was. What was it? Oh, never mind, I can't remember now. I guess I'll just enjoy the rainbow!

12.
(The Truth about) Sidewalks and Monkeys and Beets, Oh My

A group I belong to selected this writing prompt for the month of June: "Things I Know to Be True." You'd think at my advanced age, I could rattle off a few, but I am terrified to commit any of my "truths" to paper because of beets. Yes, beets.

Until about ten years ago, I "knew" that I hated beets. I'd never actually tasted a beet, mind you, but in 40-some years of living I'd never had occasion to revisit my childhood belief that beets were slices of vampire heart. At least not until I was held captive at a three-day conference where the lunches were meager and the dinner entrees took forever to be served. By the final evening, with only a salad plate of Vlad the Impaler's heart standing between me and starvation, I broke down and took a bite. My so-called truth dissolved into deliciousness right then and there. It turns out I really like beets.

Now, I might be inclined to dismiss the beets issue as an amusing holdover from childhood that managed to bypass adult re-evaluation if it were an isolated incident, but it's not. Check out these two stunning examples of adult asleep-at-the-wheel syndrome, from which I apparently suffer.

1. I believed those were real monkeys in *The Wizard of Oz*.
Okay, you probably did too...when you were eight. I was in my early thirties before the light bulb went on for me. I first saw *The Wizard of Oz* when I was in first grade and, even though on the whole I loved it, I never watched it again for the rest of my childhood because the Wicked Witch's monkey henchmen had so traumatized me. More than two decades had passed before I re-examined the monkeys through the lens of adulthood when I bought the VHS tape for my daughter's

eighth birthday. As I was wrapping it, I actually said to my husband, "Looking back now, I'm amazed those monkeys could be trained to do all those things." My husband laughed, thinking that I was being facetious, and only at that very moment did I realize that, of course, the monkeys were not monkeys at all, but people in costumes. (And some darn convincing pre-*Planet of the Apes* make-up, in my opinion.)

2. I believed a blade of grass could break through concrete in its quest to find sunlight.
One day when I was a little girl, I was standing outside with my father as he stooped down to examine a crack in the sidewalk. A slender sprig of grass had sprouted right in the middle of the crack. Pulling it out, he smiled up at me and said, "Can you believe a little blade of grass broke this hard concrete?" Not only did I believe it then, I continued to believe it until last summer. In an instance of delayed déjà vu, my husband stooped down to examine a crack in our driveway. As he pulled up the few shoots of grass growing there, I repeated the words my father had spoken to me so many years before. Different husband this time, but the same response—he laughed, thinking I was joking. Half a second later, it dawned on me that, of course, the crack preceded the grass, not vice versa. (Grass, however determined, does not actually possess superhero strength. Tree roots are a different, expensive story!)

I'm shaking my head right along with you, wondering how I could have thought such absurd things for so long. But, the key point here is that I hadn't been actively thinking them all that time. My initial (erroneous) beliefs were formed in childhood and then lay dormant in the deep recesses of my mind. They flew under the radar of conscious thought for years, just waiting for an opportunity to spring forth and publicly humiliate me. So you can see why I'm reluctant to proclaim with any real conviction the "things I know to be true." And maybe that's not such a bad thing. Maybe the only thing I really know to be true is that we need to re-examine our long-held and deep, dark "truths" from time to time to see if they hold up when exposed to the light. Especially ones like, "All people from _____ are _____." Or "If you _____, you are a _____ person." Or how about "My child would never _____."

I hope I don't have any half-baked notions of the hurtful variety tucked away in some mental closet, but I plan to remain vigilant about rooting them out just in case. In the meantime, I will leave you with this one truth that experience has unfortunately shown me to be100% valid: Stretch marks are forever. And, bonus truth here, so is cellulite.

I have to run now because I'm expecting a couple flying monkeys for lunch and I haven't finished making the beet salad yet!

13.
Animal Magnetism

Animal magnetism. Some of us have it and some of us don't. It's the luck of the draw, and at the risk of sounding immodest, I drew to an inside straight on this one. I've got animal magnetism in spades.

In my life, I have been stalked by an amorous pigeon—there were witnesses, okay—mocked by contentious squirrels and head-pecked by a deranged blackbird. But nothing compares to my first magnetic experience, which occurred when I was a teenager.

Back then, my bedroom was on the second floor and my parents' was on the first. My older sisters were grown and gone, leaving Nervous Nelly me to sleep upstairs alone. One night I awoke with a start to the sound of heavy, plodding footsteps on the roof. Had Santa, weary of battling winter storms, started delivering presents in June, I wondered. The footsteps paced back and forth directly above my bed for several minutes, sounding less like jolly old St. Nick and more like homicidal escaped-convict St. Nick with each deliberate step. Completely unnerved, I bolted out of bed and fled to the safety of the first floor guest room across the hall from my parents.

The next morning, my mother pooh-poohed my fears that a psycho off-season Santa was stomping around on the roof.

"It's probably a couple of chipmunks," she said dismissively.

"Yes, diet drop-out chipmunks, wearing steel-toed boots," I replied sarcastically. "It's clearly an axe murderer, and I am not sleeping up there."

For the next week, I inhabited my room as usual until bedtime when I would then repair to the security of the downstairs guest room. One evening, well before the witching hour had struck, my parents went out and I sat alone at my bedroom vanity, peering into my Clairol Lighted Make-Up Mirror. Suddenly, I had the eerie feeling that I was not alone. I looked up from the mirror, turned my head and—*dun, dun, duuun*—came face to face with my stalker, one fat, wiry-haired, particularly unattractive possum. His long, fleshy nose was pressed hard against my window and his beady eyes were trained unflinchingly on me. I sat frozen for a moment and then ran downstairs, screaming like a banshee.

Thus began my summer of terror at the hands—well, paws—of the peeping tom possum. He not only continued to spy on me and lope around the roof at night, he sought me out in person, once practically hurling himself in front of my car (and hurling is not something that comes easily to possums). And another time he positioned himself between me and my front door. It was horrifying, and I suffered from PTSD (Possum Traumatic Stress Disorder) for quite some time.

Now forty years later, flashbacks of that disturbing period of my life have returned. The other night my dog Harper was in the backyard when he began barking wildly, frantically, like he'd never barked before. I opened the door and repeatedly commanded him to stop. He not only ignored me, he ramped the barking up a notch. Frustrated, I grabbed a flashlight and went outside to retrieve him. Just as I grabbed hold of his collar, I sensed movement atop the fence behind me. I swung the flashlight around and caught a flash of beady eyes and fleshy nose receding into the darkness. I yanked Harper's collar and hightailed it back inside the house.

"What was it?" my husband asked as I turned the dead bolt on the back door.

Barely able to speak for shaking, I simply replied, "Well, it was no chipmunk."

Animal magnetism in spades. Trust me, it's a hand better left undealt.

14.
Preemptive Rudeness

If unassertiveness training ever catches on, I will be hailed as the exalted Grand Poobah of the movement. I pride myself on my complete inability to be forceful, firm or aggressive. I am the woman who once fired a grossly incompetent house cleaner (whose idea of thorough cleaning was to flush the toilet after dumping her cigarette butts in it) with these harsh words: "Um, Wendy, I was wondering if, like, maybe you could not work here anymore. I mean, I'd still continue to pay you every week, of course, but, like, could you just not show up?"

Still, it's not as if I have never had my moments of setting people straight. I am the essence of compliance...unless and until, that is, I encounter an act of what I call preemptive rudeness, i.e., when someone rudely warns me about my behavior before I even exhibit any behavior at all or have half a second to self-correct an inadvertent offense. Then I pretty much go off.

The incident that sort of set the bar for me in that regard occurred several years ago in West Virginia. I was minding my own business, unobtrusively making my way to my seat in a large sports arena, when my purse slipped off my shoulder and I stopped *momentarily* to reposition it. Instantly, a large, hairy, utterly unattractive boor bellowed, "More your ass. Ain't no way you gonna stand there all night blocking my view."

I was stunned! Why, it was as if he had read my mind, as that was exactly what I had planned—to pay top dollar for a ticket and then stand mid-aisle, holding my heavy coat, purse, a large diet Coke and a bag of chips for two hours straight. What could be a more enjoyable way to watch a basketball game?

I turned around, went nose-to-nose with the drunken, grammatically-challenged behemoth, and sputtered through clenched teeth, "First of all, I have no intention of standing here all night, as I, unlike you, know what is appropriate behavior in public. I merely stopped for half a second to adjust my purse. Second of all, if by chance I were to accidentally block your view for an extended period of time, the proper way to call that to my attention would be to say, 'Excuse me, *ma'am*, would you mind stepping out of the way so that I can see.' And I would immediately apologize and oblige you. That's called civil discourse. And right now, I think you should both thank me for enlightening you and apologize for your brutish behavior. Go on, I'm listening."

I would like to say he had an etiquette epiphany right then and there, but in actuality he just yelled at my husband, "You better git yer woman outta my face before I commence to punching her lights out."

For an unassertive person, I have delivered a respectable number of dressing-downs for preemptive rudeness, including to a haughty assistant bank manager, an officious clerk in the county records office and, what may have been my crowning achievement, a self-important optometrist with a bad nose job. I mention all of this now because just this afternoon I had a run-in with an offender that really raised my ire.

It was a lovely late winter afternoon in Atlanta, made lovelier by the fact that I had the day off. I stopped at Panera to grab a salad and was looking forward to eating out on the sunny patio and just enjoying the preview of spring weather. Only one other person was sitting out there, a woman at the opposite end whose back was turned to me. I set my tray on the table and myself on the chair, reached into my purse to retrieve my phone to check movie times and INADVERTENTLY touched a pop-up ad. The audio played for less than a millisecond, no, less than a microsecond, no, truly less than a nanosecond, before I stopped it.

Suddenly, the air was filled with what can only be described as a primal growl, "Noooooo! Oh, no you don't, not on my birthday! You are not coming out here and playing that thing on my birthday!"

I was so startled I jumped in my seat a bit and looked around, trying to determine where the unnatural sound was coming from. I finally figured out it was coming from the woman at the other end of the patio who still had her back turned to me. As she continued her guttural grumbling, never once turning in my direction, I further figured out she was talking to me. (Never mind that her ridiculous rant was several seconds longer, several decibels louder and infinitely more disturbing to the peace than my nanosecond breach of phone etiquette had been.) I was so taken aback, my natural unassertive/apologetic reflexes kicked in.

"I'm so sorry. I accidentally touched an audio ad on my phone. I had no intention of playing anything out here," I gushed, although by the end of my apology, I was feeling my stomach acid starting to churn in recognition of what was clearly an incident of preemptive rudeness.

Did she graciously accept my olive branch, perhaps even acknowledge with a smile that she had spoken too soon and too strongly? No! She continued in a mad, rambling monologue— addressed to the parking lot, I guess, as she still hadn't turned around to face me—about her birthday, some damn idiots, cellular noise and her not taking it anymore.

At that point, I determined that this was not a simple case of preemptive rudeness, but one with complications of full-on looniness. An act of assertiveness in this instance might well have ended with my being stabbed in the eye with a salad fork. I picked up my tray and purse and repaired to the safety of an inside table.

"I can't believe you came back inside on this gorgeous day," said one of the employees who knows me and my penchant for eating outside in any weather short of a blizzard.

"Well, there's a birthday party going on out there and I didn't want to intrude," I explained.

"There is?" she asked, confused.

"Yeah, a small party, a party of one, actually," I replied. "And trust me, the guest list is one you don't want to be on."

Looking out at the beautiful blues skies and sunshine that I was being forced to enjoy through glass, I muttered under my breath, "Happy damn birthday, you loon."

Call me unassertive if you must, but sometimes it's best to let mad dogs lie.

15.
Two of a Kind—I'm Becoming My Husband

I've often heard that over time married couples begin to resemble each other. Aside from the two whiskers that recently sprouted to the right of my upper lip, I have not noticed my appearance sliding in my husband's direction. Now I would not mind one bit if my relaxed-fit midlife thighs morphed into his muscular ones without my even having to mouth the word "Pilates," though I probably would shave them. Well, in the summer, anyway.

More concerning, however, is the new behavior I have sprouted. All my adult life I have been a staunch opponent of the recliner for two reasons. 1) Despite Brooke Shields' best attempts, I could never completely erase from my mind the image of the bulky '70s Herculon models that were anathema to my home decorating sensibilities. And 2) Recliners always represented to me old people dozing and drooling. I'm a huge fan of the nap, which is what a couch is for. Lie down and sleep like you mean it, dammit. Commit! But dozing off and on in a recliner, jaw gaping open, with a dried saliva streak down your chin—well, in my mind that was the stuff of nursing home nightmares.

For years I held the line against my first husband's desire for a recliner in which to plant himself to watch racing on TV. Maybe that's why the marriage broke up, although I think it had more to do with his secretly quitting his job, losing all our money and subsequently running off with a stripper. But who knows, my anti-recliner stance could have been a contributing factor.

At any rate, I'm talking now about my present husband, whose sleep switch is activated the instant his butt touches down in an armchair in front of the TV. For the first few years of our marriage, I tried to ignore his armchair "dozing," wherein his head would loll about from side to side, bob forward, chin to chest, and then violently jerk backwards, accompanied by a startled slurping sound each time. This became his nightly ritual, and not only did it drive me nuts, I also began to fear that one of those times his head would snap right off like the end of green bean.

I had to face the music and admit that it was time for a recliner. I turned to the internet and was pleased to find that Brooke was not joking when she touted the stylishness of the modern-day La-Z-Boy furniture lines. High style indeed, with a high price tag to match. Eventually, though, I found a recliner whose style and price fit my taste and budget, and I ordered it to surprise my husband.

As pleased as he was, the biggest surprise has been on me. I gave the chair a short test-drive the first day to check its comfort, but readily handed the keys over to my husband. Then a curious thing began to happen. Arriving home before my husband each day, I found myself drawn to the recliner to watch the early news, as it was so conveniently situated in front of the TV. I felt a bit conspicuous at first, but little by little became more at ease (which is, after all, the point of this piece of furniture). After about a week of sitting upright, I thought how silly it was to have a recliner and not, well, recline, so I did it. One push and my torso magically tilted back and my feet lifted up, effortlessly and at the perfect angle. It was comfort heaven, and I felt a little giddy with the thrill of it all.

This became my secret ritual for a few weeks until the unthinkable happened—I dozed off! In the recliner! And my husband came home and caught me, drool-faced and snoring! Oh, the shame and endless ridicule I endured. But, long story short, I am now rearranging the furniture to accommodate the second recliner I have on order. I've also ordered a pack of drool bibs. The process of merging two spouses into one has undeniably begun, and I'm really okay with it. I've accepted the two whiskers, and I've even accepted that I am a drooling dozer. Now if only my thighs would get with the program!

16.
A Squirrely Situation: Vindication Is Finally Mine

I am not a vengeful person, at least not an overly vengeful one. True, I stifled a snicker when I heard an old flame's hair was thinning as quickly as his waist was thickening, but it's not like I had wished that on him. I just took a *teensy* bit of delight in it. No matter how unjustly I think I've been treated, I am usually content with allowing karma to take care of things—if only because I fear seeking revenge would only heap bad karma back on me.

But let me tell you, vindication is a whole different matter. I did not actively seek it out, but after enduring more than twenty years of ridicule, doubts and eye rolls, vindication has found me. And it is sweet.

My traumatic tale began twenty-five years, four houses, three dogs and one marriage ago. My husband, daughter and I had just completed a much-anticipated move to a new city and I'd spent the whole morning cleaning—and reveling in—our brand spanking new house. It was perfect. After lunch, I settled into a cushioned lounge chair on the deck for a short break. It was a glorious fall day, bright blue skies, gold and crimson leaves gently rustling on the trees that framed the deck. As the autumn sun warmed my skin, a feeling of complete contentment washed over me and my eyelids became heavier and heavier. I was just giving myself over to a delicious slumber when it happened.

A loud *ker-plunk, ker-plunk* sounded on the deck beside my head and startled me. I sat up, looked around and saw two large acorns beside my chair. Oh, I thought, I guess they fell out of the tree. Just as I was resettling myself and closing my eyes, *ker-plunk, ker-plunk, ker-plunk,* three more acorns landed beside me and rolled under the lounge chair. And then *ker-plunk, ker-plunk, ker-plunk,* another three immediately followed.

45

My interest piqued, I sat up with eyes wide open, waiting to see if the shelling would continue. Within seconds a veritable barrage of acorns rained down on me from the biggest oak tree. Looking up, I was stunned by what I saw. It wasn't the gentle breeze liberating the acorns from the tree, but two squirrely squirrels!

"What's the big idea?" I yelled up at them.

"*Squeak-squawk-squeeeeak,*" they replied in a smart-alecky tone. (Not necessarily smart-alecky for middle schoolers, mind you, but pretty darn smart-alecky for squirrels.) I swear they were up there elbowing each other, proud that they'd gotten one over on the human.

Thus began the squirrel wars. For the next few years I was regularly pelted with acorns, small twigs and clumps of dried leaves whenever I stepped out onto the deck alone. One morning, they even dropped a hunk of French bread on me, which I assume they pilfered from the trash of one of the nearby restaurants, although it's possible they had their own little bakery up there. If so, I hoped a *macaron* bomb was headed my way.

To make matters worse, my only witness to this rodent roguery was my dog Ruckus, whom those delinquents mercilessly taunted by hanging from the tree just out of her reach, causing her to go completely berserk with frustration. I shared that sentiment. With the two of us the sole victims—and Ruckus not all that verbal—it was impossible to convince anyone else of my waking nightmare. My own daughter rolled her eyes and asked me what I'd been smoking.

I tried everything I could to confuse the enemy. I'd go out at different times of day, speak in loud foreign accents and wear my daughter's old Halloween masks. All of these maneuvers took place when I was alone, of course, because that's the only time those bushy-tailed bullies struck. One afternoon, however, my husband came home early and found me standing at the window, binoculars trained on the command center, i.e., the nest at the top of the oak tree.

"What the hell are you doing?" he asked.

"What does it look like I'm doing?" I snapped impatiently. "I'm trying to read their lips to get a fix on their next move. And it's not easy because, as it turns out, squirrels have practically no lips."

He walked away, shaking his head.

The truth is I never did get the upper hand on those furry little miscreants. I don't know if it was the same squirrels year after year or if the original squirrels left instructions in their will, but the reign of terror, while it ebbed and flowed, only ended for good when we moved away.

Fast forward to this past Tuesday. I was talking to my daughter on the phone. Expecting a baby in four weeks, she and her husband had just left city living behind and bought their first house in the suburbs, one complete with an expansive deck and a yard full of trees. I was looking at the photos she had texted me and exclaimed, "Wow, that deck is beautiful!"

"Yeah, right," she snorted. "Too bad we can't use it."

"You can't use it?" I asked, confused.

"Not unless we want to get bombarded with acorns," she continued, her voice full of annoyance. "Mom, the squirrels in our yard are little jerks!"

I laughed right out loud.

"Mom, I'm serious. They're complete jerks! They hit my friend on the head the other day and she said it really hurt. A baby could get a concussion out there!"

I tried to remind her about my experience, but she was on a rodent roll and talked right over me. And that was fine. I didn't need her to acknowledge what I'd been through or apologize for not believing me all those years ago. The chickens had come home to roost—right alongside the squirrels—and that was good enough for me. After all, I thought with satisfaction, I am not a vengeful person.

17.
Nailing Addiction (and kicking my bi-weekly habit to the curb)

My story isn't new. You've likely heard heartbreaking tales of everyday people who got in over their heads, who thought they could control their habit and found out too late their habit completely controlled them. Addiction long ago migrated from back alleys to Main Street America. And still the thought that someone like I was at the time, an everyday wife and mother, could get sucked into that vortex of destruction might seem hard to believe. But I did get sucked in. Off and on for more than twenty years, I was using. Now much older, a bit wiser and more than a year into recovery, I'm sharing my sordid tale in hopes of sparing others needless suffering.

Hello, my name is Lee and I'm an acrylic nail-aholic.

It all started with an innocent curiosity—such a cliché, I know. Acrylic nails weren't even on my radar the day my neighbor, another young PTA mom, sat on my couch and pulled back the curtain on a lifestyle that at once frightened and fascinated me. She talked about how acrylics, with their uniform size and ridge-free surface, made her feel more confident and self-assured. There had been days in the past, she confessed, when she'd felt too self-conscious about her raggedy nails to even serve the coffee at a PTA meeting, much less raise her hand to vote. But, no more, she said, not since she'd begun using. She was a "hands on" kind of gal now, she crowed.

"Okay, take your nails, for example," she continued, examining my fingertips. "They grow to a decent length, but they peel and split and then you're right back to stubs again. Don't you deserve more from life than stubs?"

"I guess so," I replied nervously. "I mean, maybe. Oh, I don't know—what will people think?"

"Look around," she said with authority. "All the moms are doing it. And you didn't hear it from me, but even Taylor's first grade teacher is hooked. She has a standing appointment at Nail Jazz every other Friday. The owner herself told me."

I'd like to blame it all on peer pressure, but the truth is that I was weak. I'd been struggling to a achieve a certain level of nail perfection for years—always falling short, of course—and the notion of a quick fix was enormously appealing to me. And once I started, I felt powerless to stop, despite the time and money the bi-weekly fill-ins siphoned from my life, and even despite the threat of permanent damage to my nail bed.

I swear if I tried to quit once, I tried a hundred times. But with a nail salon on every corner, offering discounts on full sets and half-price on fill-ins, I inevitably ended up with that wretched monkey—albeit one with beautifully manicured nails—on my back again. Until New Year's Day 2015, that is. When the clock struck midnight on January 1, 2015, I made a resolution to go cold turkey and, thanks to my higher power, also known as my husband who dared me to do it, I've been acrylic-free for nineteen months.

It hasn't been easy. Every time I go for a pedicure, those wily nail techs try to lure me in. Try the gel polish, they coo. It wears without chipping or peeling, they say. It's just a little polish, nothing to be afraid of, they tease, wagging their gelled-up nails in my face.

Oh, get thee behind me, Satan! Nothing to be afraid of? Make no mistake, gel polish is a gateway drug to the hard polymers and those salon seductresses know it!

And that's the bottom line here, folks. That's the ugly truth hiding under the glamorous surface of those acrylic tips. They may seem like your savior in the short run, but they will destroy you in the long run. Take your money elsewhere. Get your mustache waxed, have an extra Starbucks or just save it for a rainy day. And if you're ever tempted to go down the polymer path to hell, remember these words, my friends: Nothing real can come from false nails.

18.
Pooped Out

I am pooped out. Literally. No, really, I literally mean literally pooped out. You see, I had a colonoscopy this morning, which required me to spend all day yesterday "prepping" for it. That means that in the past 36 hours, a heck of a lot more has come out of me than has gone in. In fact, post-procedure, the only thing I'm full of right now is air, although even that is beginning to make its way out of me and I am very grateful that I am home alone.

As humiliating medical procedures go, a colonoscopy ranks right up there, but it does have a few things going for it in my opinion. For one, it is an equal opportunity humiliater. Unlike the mammogram and pelvic exam, which assault parts only women have, a colonoscopy is no respecter of gender. Both the object of its scrutiny as well as its point of entry are, like opinions, things everyone has.

Second, you at least get some pay-off for the crappy prep day in the form of a wonderful, drug-induced nap. As both a skilled napper and a veteran of four "scopings," I speak with some authority when I say this is one of the highest quality naps your insurance dollars can buy. You are out immediately and completely, no tossing, no turning, no counting of sheep. True, you are violated with a couple feet of flexible tubing while you are asleep, but that seems a fair exchange, especially if it gets you out of work for a day or two.

Third, as unpleasant as the prep process is, when it's over, you feel oddly invigorated—once the post-anesthesia goofiness passes, that is. You are, intestinally speaking, as clean as a whistle, purged of all the debris that was weighing you down, and ready to make a fresh start. The physical sensation of newness might even motivate you to renew commitments in other areas of your life. You could use the prep process as a sort of reset button for all your flagging New Year's resolutions. Or you could just use it to justify eating a pint of chocolate gelato the next day; that's good, too.

With a family history of colon cancer, I take regular colonoscopies very seriously. Getting hit from behind, so to speak, every few years is a small price to pay for preventing a deadly disease. Even so, such an intimate encounter, especially the first time around, can leave you and your dignity feeling a little compromised. A bit embarrassed after his initial experience, my friend told his doctor, "Jeez, you could at least offer to take me to lunch after that." Yes, and cab fare home with a promise to call soon would be nice gestures as well, but dream on. Such expectations are unrealistic in today's "stick 'em and street 'em" society, so, you just gotta put on—well, take off, actually— your big girl panties/big boy pants and roll over on your side.

My doctor may never have bought me lunch or supplied my cab fare, but she has given me many a reassuring hug as well as her word that together she and I are doing all the right things to keep my bowels unobstructed and open for business. And, occasionally, like today, she even gives me a little bonus. Waking from my propofol slumber this morning, I found tucked into my hand a special reminder of our time together—a souvenir photograph of my internal hemorrhoid. Now that alone, my friends, was worth the price of submission!

19.
Mirror, Mirror, Who's the Oldest of Them All?

They say you should never believe your own press, that you are neither as great nor as awful as any particular source deems you to be. I just had that lesson slap me in the face. Hard. Some of the young women—in their 20s and 30s—from my adult ESL class hung around after class this morning and we started talking about age and how fast time flies. I happen to have a "milestone" (or as I often think of it, a 100,000-mile-stone) birthday coming up this summer and I mentioned that I couldn't believe I was going to be that age. They mistakenly understood me to say "forty-six" and spontaneously exclaimed, "Forty-six isn't *that* old. You look great."

Forty-six, old? Are you kidding me? I mean, are you even potty trained yet at forty-six? I'm pretty sure I was still sucking my thumb. The fantasy of being forty-six again was so intoxicating that I was tempted to let their gross misunderstanding (and obvious nearsightedness and/or brown-nosing) slide, but I fessed up and corrected them.

"Ladies, check your ears or your English. I said SIX-ty, SIX-ZERO, not forty-SIX."

Now, I am not delusional enough to think they really believed I looked 46, but I do believe they were sincerely surprised at my real age, as evidenced by their immediate close-up, hands-on examination of my skin to look for wrinkles and check for elasticity. (Not to mention the ringleader urging the students hanging back to step up and do the same.) The women in my family do tend to have faces that belie their age—my 35-year-old daughter still gets carded—so I am a bit fortunate in that genetic regard. From the neck down, however, the illusion begins to deteriorate, at least in my case. One peek in the dressing room after the Spanx and duct tape have been peeled off and you'll start measuring me for a pine box.

Nevertheless, I left class and headed to the supermarket with a little extra bounce in my step from the temporary ego boost. Make that very temporary. When I got to the check-out line, the cashier, without a second's hesitation, automatically applied the senior citizen discount right to my supposed younger-than-my-years face. My heart sank, yes, just like everything below my waist already has.

And this is the problem with basing our worth on others' opinions. We go from the heights to the depths inside of fifteen minutes and, in truth, neither extreme may be particularly accurate. Ideally, the only estimation of our value that should matter, from our greatness to our awfulness, is our own. That's why it's called self-worth and not imputed-to-me-by-the-judgment-of-others-worth. Plus, that would be really hard to say.

But here's the thing, sometimes it's our own internal assessment that is off. Sometimes our internal mirror is the one reflecting the distorted image. What then? That's when we need someone outside of ourselves to hold up a mirror that reflects a clear image for us. Many of us tend to undervalue ourselves and we need someone to hold up what my friend Jeanie calls the mirror of perfection to us. And at other times, we may need someone to gently, but honestly let us know where we're going off course and help us get back on the right track.

In the end, we have to weigh and balance the messages coming from within and those coming from without. We have to listen to our own voice and sometimes the voices of others that we trust and then decide what feels right for us. We are the only ones who determine our truth. And I have just determined I'm going with my students' generous opinion as my truth for today. But I'm keeping the senior discount, baby!

20.
The Overlooked Value of Occasional Inauthenticity

I'm writing this at 6:15 on All Hallows' Eve. Very soon princesses, pirates, witches and werewolves will be upon my doorstep. I can't wait to oooh and aaah over each costume, feigning shock and amazement that such exotic creatures have suddenly, inexplicably materialized right here in my sedate suburban cul-de-sac. Halloween is one of the few times when we are actually encouraged to conceal our true identities. We purposely don disguises and hide behind masks and make-up to mislead others about who we are. On Halloween, we strive to present ourselves to the world as just about anyone but our authentic selves.

That certainly flies in the face of the prevailing wisdom about how to achieve success on the other days of the year. In the buzz-wordy parlance of self-help gurus, relationship experts and career strategists, finding genuine fulfillment in life comes down to exactly just that—authenticity. We're urged to drop our masks, to be our true authentic selves and speak our true authentic message in our true authentic voice. In the quest for the ideal self-image, life partner or client, real is in and fake is out (with eyelashes, boobs and hair color being apparent exceptions).

Now, far be it from me to advocate leading a life of complete hypocrisy, but I think being inauthentic is getting short shrift here. There have been more times than I can count when being just a little less than genuine has saved everything from my pride to my employment. The judicious use of masks is what makes it possible for us to endure certain people and certain circumstances without leaving a trail of casualties in our wake.

Can you really imagine surviving holiday dinners with some of your once-removed-but-unfortunately-grown-back relatives without your fake enjoyment mask? Or how about listening to a five-year-old recount her flying monkey dream—*and, um, it was like a monkey, but it wasn't a real monkey, but it still looked like a monkey*—without your fake fascination mask? And I know for a fact that I would have never survived my term of indentured servitude—eight years of teaching middle school—without my "it's-an-absolute-joy-to-have-your-child-in-my-class-despite-the-fact-that-he-chews-with-his-mouth-open-and-once-threw-a-chair-at-me" mask.

So, on this holiday when we celebrate being who we're not, let's remember that a little inauthenticity now and then isn't such a bad thing any time of year. Grab a mask and repeat after me, "You look like you've lost weight, I love your new haircut, and velour is definitely making a comeback."

And, of course, I meant almost every word of that.

Happy Inauthentic Halloween!

21.
Sex, Drugs and Metamucil

Ladies and gentlemen, we have been betrayed! Forget all the nonsense the medical establishment has fed you about healthy living and longevity. It's all been a pack of lies and I have proof. The Rolling Stones, with an average age higher than the members of the U.S. Supreme Court, are still touring in this, the year 2017 of the Common Era.

How is it possible that Sir Michael Philip Jagger, age 74, is still whirling like a dervish while I can't tie my orthopedic shoes without triggering a muscle spasm? Take one look at him gyrating across the stage and then tell me how a lifetime regimen of sex, drugs and rock 'n' roll can be bad for you. He's still got the moves like Jagger, whereas I, the clean-living one, have the moves like someone playing a deranged version of Twister, awkwardly maneuvering to accommodate my plantar fasciitis, sciatica and positional vertigo.

Well, starting today, I am getting serious about my health. To be honest, when I was much younger, I did play around a little with better living through sex, drugs—well, alcohol, anyway—and rock 'n' roll, but I realize that if you want real progress, you need to be consistent over time. So, I am committing to Mick's three-pronged approach. Of course, I understand that coming late to the party as I am, I may need to make some adjustments to his rigorous routine.

Adjustment #1, Sex: It will be limited to one partner, my husband. And my husband will sadly confirm that many nights I am so tired it would take a lot more than the Rolling Stones to start me up. As for physical limitations, again, expectations must be adjusted downward. These days I believe I would need lumbar support for phone sex.

Adjustment #2, Drugs: Okay, I am a total wash-out here, as I am probably one of three people who came of age in the last 50 years who never took any illegal substances (although, I did flirt with a pre-illegal substance, the artificial sweetener cyclamate before it was banned for causing cancer). It is unlikely that I will begin taking any hard drugs now unless, of course, Metamucil counts, in which case, I'm in deep. That leaves alcohol, a substance which I did use in my younger days, but apparently not in sufficient quantities to benefit from its preservative properties as was obviously the case with Sir Mick. Most of my alcohol consumption nowadays comes in the form of Nyquil.

Adjustment #3, Rock 'n' Roll: I am pretty good on this front, although it was recently pointed out to me that I should check my Spotify playlists for expiration dates. I didn't realize that music had a limited shelf life, but I guess time really does keep on "slippin',slippin', slippin' into the future." Unfortunately, it seems I spend more and more time slidin', slidin',slidin' into the past.

I know it is unrealistic to think that I will ever see the results that Mick Jagger has enjoyed due to a lifetime of full-strength sex, drugs and rock'n'roll, but maybe, with a little luck and determination, my watered-down plan will at least enable me to move along with him through a verse or two of "Shattered." Aw, who am I kidding? I couldn't follow his footsteps even with my new arch supports. Maybe I'll sit down for a while, give my bunions a rest and just hum along. You know, I'm feeling better already.

22.
Stuck in the Middle with Myself

I pride myself on having a wide range of female friends. And I mean wide range rather literally, as several of my girlfriends happen to be clustered at the extreme ends of the height spectrum. Over the years, I have listened sympathetically to each end gripe about the ridiculous-to-rude remarks they routinely endure, but lately it's become almost a competition about who has it worse, the under-talls or the over-talls. I feel their pain, and if your personal altitude has exposed you to unfair ridicule and mockery, I feel your pain as well. But you all are not the only ones suffering injustice on the vertical plane. Why leave me out? This is still America, gosh darn it, and I intend to claim my fair share of victimhood.

Now hear this: middle dwellers suffer too. We are your mothers, your sisters and your daughters, although it's likely you never noticed us as we blend into the crowd without distinction. We of nondescript height are neither charmingly petite nor alluringly statuesque. We are stuck in the middle, part of the pack, just one of the herd. If height were hair color, we'd be dishwater blond. If height were grades, we'd be a "C" average. We are neither rare, nor well-done; we are plainly and unremarkably medium. Medium, a breath away from mediocre.

We are the usual; you are the unusual. We are the typical; you are the atypical. We are the expected; you are the exceptional. Let's face it, we average-heighters put the ordinary in extraordinary. Even the Bible eschews those of us who occupy the middle ground. It says we, the lukewarm, being neither hot nor cold, will be spit out of God's mouth. Spit out of the mouth of the Almighty (who presumably made us this way in the first place!). That's a bit more severe than having to suffer foolish comments like "How's the weather up there?" or "You don't have far to go when you fall down."

You, both the height-gifted and the height-challenged, command attention wherever you go. Heads turn and tongues wag when you walk in a room because you are, folks say, "something to see." The most people say about us middle-of-the-roaders, if they say anything at all, is that we are nothing to write home about. So, tall ones and small ones, be grateful for your major or minor stature. It accords you recognition we fair-to-middling types will never attain. Tiptoes can never lift me high enough nor slouching push me low enough to be of note, a status you achieve just by being who you are. And who better to be other than yourself?

Come to think of it, who better for any of us—high, low or somewhere in between—to be other than ourselves? I hereby declare the height-whining competition null and void. (But I still think I should have won.)

23.
Wanted: High-Tech Granny; Engineering Degree Required

I am about one month away from my grandmother midterm test, and I don't mind telling you I am a little nervous. In January I had to study harder than an insurance adjuster before a personality test to pass the entrance exam. Back then I prepared to keep my two-month-old granddaughter by myself for a few days by poring over operating manuals until I was bleary-eyed, trying to master all the high-tech baby gizmos that have become *de rigueur* these days. From video monitoring systems more sophisticated than NASA's to car seats-cum-strollers equipped with enough levers to control the output of the Hoover Dam, it was all pretty intimidating for this low-tech grandma.

Good grief, back in the dark ages of the early '80s, I had a wind-up swing, a bath sponge and an umbrella stroller for my infant daughter and thought myself well outfitted. Not so nowadays. Of course, nowadays, gender reveal parties, extravagant PBV's (Pre-Birth Vacations), and push presents are also the over-the-top norm. The closest I got to a push present in 1982 was the wad of tissues a nurse handed me when I thought I might lose control of my bowels during labor. But, you know, at least I'm not bitter.

Before my daughter left the baby with me in January, she put me through my paces, and, good student that I am, I passed with flying colors. I juggled Boppies and binkies, buckled and unbuckled safety harnesses and seat belts, and converted the car seat into a stroller and back into a car seat again. I even debated the benefits of the Baby K'tan versus the Baby Bjorn. All without missing a beat.

And, not to brag, but after a mere seventeen straight hours of research on the internet, I picked out and purchased—without my daughter's supervision—not only a Pack 'n' Play with Reversible Napper and Changer Bassinet, but also a Papasan Cradle Swing with floating butterfly mobile, light show and soothing music. Yeah, drop the mic, baby. The Fisher-Price mic, that is.

But now I'm nervous that such pride goeth before a fall as the grandmother midterm loometh on the horizon. Of course, I am tickled baby-girl pink to be keeping my granddaughter for two weeks in July, but everything I learned in January is useless because all that infant equipment is pretty much obsolete for her at eight months. Now it's all about Bumbo seats, ExerSaucers and GoPods. And, of course, the car seat has completely different settings now. Oh, dear, can an old dog like me learn even more new tricks?

I have a stack of owner's manuals, complete with schematics, color illustrations and customer reviews, piled high on my bedside table. I keep telling myself *I can do this, I must do this, it's for the baby*. But, to be perfectly honest, I'm exhausted just thinking about it. If I could find an adult-sized Rock 'n' Play somewhere, I'd curl up in its extra deep and cozy seat right now and let its hands-free, soothing rocking motion and twelve calming melodies lull me into heavenly, high-tech slumber. Zzzzzz.

24.
No Free Lunch

Early in our courtship, my now husband invited me to lunch at a Colombian restaurant. I knew a little about Colombian food, but was anxious to try more dishes under the expert guidance of my new boyfriend from Bogota, Jorge.

The server brought the menus, and she and Jorge exchanged pleasantries in Spanish while I said *Gracias* a lot and nodded vigorously. Everything sounded so wonderfully exotic that I wanted to try it all, but didn't want to leave Jorge with a huge check so early in the dating game—or myself with split seams. Jorge, however, insisted that I get a good sampling of Colombian fare, and he rattled off a list of delicacies we had to have.

I left my "modest" order for *arroz con pollo*, beans, salad and sweet plantains with Jorge and ran to the restroom. Tall glasses of *sorbete de lulo* and *limonada de coco* were being set down at our table as I walked away. Lord only knows what gastronomic pleasures I'll find on the table when I return, I thought to myself.

When I came back, I asked Jorge what he had ordered for himself. He answered, "A bowl of soup."

"And what else?" I asked.

"Nothing, that's enough for me," he replied casually.

What was going on, I wondered. Why had he suddenly changed his tune and only ordered soup while insisting I have more in one sitting than I normally have in a whole week? Was it some kind of trick to see how big my appetite was? The more I pressed him about only having soup, the more reticent he became. Oh, dear, I thought, maybe he forgot his wallet and is too embarrassed to say so. Before I could say another word, the waitress was at the table, depositing heaping plates of food—on my side.

"You'll have to help me eat all of this," I said, embarrassed by my bounty and his glaring lack thereof.

Just then I saw the waitress heading back to our table, visibly struggling under the weight of a tray laden with yet more food. I was about to protest when she unloaded every bit of it in front of Jorge. The centerpiece was a large soup bowl—actually, more like a tureen.

"What is all this?" I asked, confused.

"It's my soup," Jorge replied and burst out laughing.

That was my introduction to *Sancocho Colombiano*, a buffet in a bowl that has about as much in common with regular soup as cheese has with cheesecake. I watched in amazement as he pulled out what seemed like a side of beef, a pork roast and at least half a chicken from the bowl and put them on his plate to cut them up. Even without the meat, the bowl of savory broth was still filled to the brim with chunks of potato, yucca and sizable pieces of corn on the cob. And as if that wasn't enough food to sink a ship, it was served with sides of rice, avocado and a salad.

"Just a bowl of soup, huh, *Señor*?" I asked him sarcastically. "And to think I was worried that you'd forgotten your wallet and were afraid to tell me. I was trying to figure out how I could offer to pay without embarrassing you, you big, fat Colombian liar!"

He downright guffawed at that and said he knew better. "Everyone knows there is no such thing as a free lunch, *querida*. Not in Colombia and not in the United States."

I was reminiscing about this incident last weekend after my debacle of a Father's Day celebration for Jorge (whom I eventually married, despite the soup prank). I am well known for my event-planning capabilities, pulling off elaborate themes and schemes to mark all occasions, from birthdays to anniversaries to nail clippings. This year I had planned a series of surprises for Jorge, every single one of which, incredibly, blew up in my face. If it could go wrong, it did, and Father's Day morning found me unexpectedly facing my husband empty-handed. I was so disappointed, but he took it all in good-natured stride.

I ended up taking him out to an altogether unspectacular place for lunch and despite all my missteps for the day, we had a lovely time. Right up until the check arrived. I reached into my purse for my wallet, and panic shot through me. I remembered I had locked my wallet in the glove compartment of my car when I had gone to the dog park earlier that morning. We had driven to the restaurant in Jorge's car.

When I told Jorge that I didn't have my wallet and that he would have to pay for his own Father's Day lunch, he asked if I had been waiting twelve years to pull this trick as payback for the *sancocho* incident. I laughed and reminded him that he was the one who bragged about knowing there was no such thing as a free lunch.

"That's true," he said, nodding his head. "Not in Colombia and not in the United States."

And not, unfortunately for him, on Father's Day either. Live and learn, friends, live and learn.

25.
Sorry, Mom . . . Again

With every year that passes, it seems I owe my mother yet another apology for doing or saying something that I, in the superior wisdom of my youth,—i.e., naiveté—once vowed I would *never, ever* do or say. So, yeah, I've been eating my words for a good 25 years now. And to add insult to injury, recent photos suggest they have been high fat, high sugar words at that.

Back in the day, I swore:

1) I would never wear any outfit past its trendiness expiration date . . . until I got my first car and found out how much snow tires cost.

2) I would never leave the house looking *like that* . . . until I stayed up all night with a feverish baby and went to work wearing one brown shoe and one black one.

3) I would never use candy to bribe a child into compliance. . .until I was stuck in a mile-long check-out line with a melting down toddler.

4) I would never lose my patience and screech ridiculous, unenforceable threats, such as grounding a child to her grave and beyond . . . until I had a teenager.

Well, you get the idea. Lots of high calorie words building up on my hips over the years. But after the stunt I pulled this morning, I'm going to be eating words roughly the caloric equivalent of a Boston cream pie. Until today, my mother's famous "drive-by incident of 1971" remained the high water mark for menopausal memory lapses in our family. That day, my 54-year-old mother was supposed to drive my friend and me to a basketball game at the junior high. My mom went out to pull the car around while my friend and I stood at the end of the sidewalk, waiting for her. Once she was in the car, my mother headed our way, but instead of stopping, she blithely drove right past us and disappeared into the night. My friend began to panic, but I calmly assured her that this sort of thing had happened before and that my mom would be back—eventually. I made no promises about making the opening tip off.

As my mom told it, once she hit the middle of town, she put her finger to her cheek and wondered aloud where she was going and why. With a little mental backtracking, she eventually remembered her passengers and returned for us. Oh, how we all howled about that for years, teasing her mercilessly every time she got behind the wheel and asking with exaggerated concern whether she'd forgotten anything—or any*one*.

And then this morning happened to me. I got in my car to run some routine errands, stopping first at the drive-thru dry cleaners that I've been going to for ten years. I pulled up and Mr. Lee, the genial owner, came out to greet me, as he does each time. We chatted a bit about holiday madness as he opened the back door to retrieve my load. Suddenly, he fell silent. Then, genuinely confused, he asked, "What do you want me to do with this?"

"Oh, just the usual light starch," I replied, a bit confused myself.

"I'm not sure that's a good idea," he said, laughing.

I turned around to see what the problem was. There on my back seat, just as pleased as punch, sat my dog Harper—and not one stitch of laundry. The light bulb went on and I remembered that I was actually on my way to the veterinarian this morning when my brain apparently went on auto-pilot and I ended up at the dry cleaners instead. (In my defense, they do advertise themselves as "fur specialists.") Mr. Lee and I had a good laugh and then I drove off in the direction of the vet's office, just shaking my head.

Thus, the drive-thru incident of 2015 has now entered the annals of Menopausal Moments. My mom has been gone nearly two years, yet I'm still regularly learning from—and apologizing to—her. Looking down on me this morning, I'm sure she had a good laugh. Surely, even in heaven, vindication must still be sweet. As for me, I went home, sat down and cut myself a big slice of humble pie. I don't suppose that's ever anyone's favorite dish, but I must say, the Boston cream isn't too bad. Next time you have to eat your words, you might want to give it a try.

26.
No Ticket to Paradise

Well, apparently I'm going to have to wait a little longer to be a billionaire. I bought two Powerball tickets for the historic $1.5 billion drawing and didn't match so much as one stinking number on either ticket. I suppose it's a good thing I didn't quit my job yesterday after all.

This was not my first brush with lottery letdown. I am hopelessly addicted to believing that life is a magical experience, chock full of meaningful coincidence and synchronicity, and I am forever looking for "signs" to guide me and confirm my beliefs. Thirty-four years ago when I gave birth to my daughter, I was certain the stars had aligned to mark this momentous occasion with a generous gift. I checked into the hospital at precisely 7:40 a.m. and gave birth exactly twelve hours later at 7:40 p.m. on...*wait for it*...04/07!

The message was clear—I was obviously being given the winning lottery numbers. I dispatched my husband to the nearest gas station to play the numbers zero, four and seven, in any order, for one week. Back in 1982, that was about as fancy as the Pennsylvania lottery got, three numbers, pulled daily. For the next seven days, I waited anxiously for the televised 6:30 drawing. Nope, not a single zero, four or seven was ever pulled that week. Apparently, the universe had decided my baby girl was gift enough, and I had to agree. She was more than enough.

I didn't give the lottery much thought again until a few years ago when, once more, I felt I was being directed by powers greater than myself to buy a scratch-off ticket. It all started one day when I stepped out of my car at the gas station. Looking down, I saw an old scratch-off lottery ticket directly under my foot. I picked it up and tossed it in the trash. The very next day, when I got out of my car at a grocery store where I didn't normally shop, another used scratch-off ticket was on the ground right beside my car. Hmm. Again, I picked it up and threw it in the trash. The third day, I was walking through the parking lot after work when what should appear in my path but yet another scratch-off ticket. Well, that was the clincher.

I immediately headed to the nearest QuikTrip and added two $5.00 scratch-off tickets to my normal purchase of diet Snapple peach iced tea. My hands shaking in anticipation of hitting it big, I took a dime out of my wallet and began scratching off each square. When all were scratched and done, the only money I was holding was my dime.

So for the past two weeks, while billionaire fever infected seemingly everyone in the nation, my temperature remained a cool-headed 98.6. And then my husband, who was out of the country at the time, called and asked if I had bought any tickets. When I told him I was beyond falling for empty promises of quick riches via a set of magic numbers, he laughed, but urged me to pick up a couple tickets for fun. After all, I'd be participating in a historic event, he argued.

The following day when I stopped at QuikTrip to satisfy my daily tea habit, I plunked down four bucks for two quick pick tickets. For the following 36 hours, I tried not to focus on the "what if" thoughts, but I couldn't help furnishing a restored Tuscan villa in my head. By the evening of the drawing, "what if" had turned into "why not," and I had pretty much settled on the design of the new swimming pool I was planning to add to my villa. Then, as both times before, my hopes were dashed. I didn't even come close, not one matching number, not one ho-hum prize, not even a measly bag of fries.

The next time I get the urge to buy a lottery ticket, I'm buying a couple extra bottles of Snapple instead. I believe a little peach iced tea could taste quite refreshing on a hot Tuscan summer day.

27.

Bye, Bye, American Pie

I would like to start by stating very clearly that I love my country and I'm all for buying American. I must also be honest, however, and admit that there are times when you have to tap the international market to get the best quality. You shop around, you do a side-by-side comparison and sometimes, from cars to computers to cardigan sweaters, you find the import stands head and shoulders above the U.S. product.

I speak from personal experience in the domestic vs. import debate regarding one item in particular, the husband. I have had one of each and I can tell you there is simply no contest. The import outperforms the domestic on every level imaginable, which is even more impressive considering I got the domestic husband straight off the showroom floor—although, in retrospect, I believe he was actually an off-lease model passed off for new—while I picked up the imported husband second-hand. But that's the difference quality materials and craftsmanship make. After all, a pre-owned Mercedes S-class will obviously deliver a much smoother ride than even a spanking new Chevy Spark. Even twelve years in, the import's motor still has plenty of zip, whereas the domestic model started dragging his tailpipe within weeks of my signing on the dotted line.

The import ticks all the expected boxes: loving, intelligent, funny and willing to carry heavy things and kill large bugs. Not to mention, his sleek exterior is quite easy on the eyes. But, more importantly, many features that the domestic model lacked completely—with disastrous consequences—came standard on the import. Fidelity, integrity and honor were all part of the import's package, no up-charge, no fine print, no exceptions.

In matters of care and handling, again, in my experience, the import takes top honors. He is the very antithesis of high maintenance. A regular supply of love and tenderness with a few Snickers bars thrown in are all it takes to keep him running in top condition. The essence of stability, he displays none of the prickly moodiness and unpredictability that plagued the shaky domestic model and often left me stranded by the wayside.

And so in this instance of domestic vs. import, the hands-down winner is the import. I realize, of course, that there are plenty of good domestic model husbands to be found out there, but, unfortunately, that was not my experience. If I have to come up with one complaint about my imported husband, it's that it took so long to find him. But, fortunately, I did and ever since his pink slip has been all mine!

28.
The Day My Leg Almost "Sploded"

I've had several dogs in my life, each with its own idiosyncrasies. There was the one who retrieved used Q-tips from the trash, the one who was afraid of wallpaper and the one who snatched a wedge of cheese right off the serving tray in the middle of a dinner party, generously leaving his half-chewed bone in its place. But until now I've never had a dog who tried to detonate one of my limbs. Enter Harper, our recently adopted Labrador mix. Mixed with what is anyone's guess, but my money is on unbridled lunacy.

The first time we took Harper to the park, he jerked the leash out of my husband's hand, leapt into the lake and attempted to navigate its full length and breadth for 45 minutes, oblivious to our frantic commands—accompanied by wild arm-flapping—to return to shore.

That's when I got the bright idea to attach a long rope to his harness, allowing him to swim while enabling us to reel in his defiant little behind, if necessary. My husband fastened the other end of the rope around his waist like a good Boy Scout and we were in business.

The plan was working well until Harper spotted another dog back on the shore. Faster than you can say *Marley and Me*, Harper launched himself out of the water and lunged in the direction of the other dog, pulling the rope tight and lashing it like a high tension wire against the back of my leg. I collapsed, yelping in pain, as my husband, propelled forward by the semi-airborne Harper, stumbled past me.

My leg instantly began swelling like a water balloon and turning a deep shade of purple. It looked as if my calf were giving birth to an overweight eggplant. I watched in horror as an engorged, steel-blue vein violently pulsated while my skin strained to contain it. I swore I could hear my skin stretching.

My formerly well-spoken Colombian husband took one look at my leg and suddenly began channeling Ricky Ricardo. "Oh my God, baby, I 'theenk' is going to 'splode!'" he exclaimed.

"Oh dear God, can that actually happen?" I cried.

Off we sped to the ER, where the doctor, barely suppressing his amusement at the circumstances of my injury, had some "splainin" to do to allay our fears. Despite the rope rupturing approximately 1.7 billion capillaries, he determined no real damage had been done. My leg would not, he assured us, "splode." It would, however, resemble an overstuffed sausage for quite some time.

Since the rope incident, I've caught Harper gazing longingly at my leg on more than one occasion. Surely, he wouldn't confuse my leg with a real sausage, would he? Ay, ay, ay, I can just imagine myself "splainin" that one at the ER.

29.
Ironing Out Second Honeymoon Wrinkles

It's a well-known fact that I'm a big proponent of "seconds"—all sorts of seconds, from second helpings (that's where my "big" came from) to second chances. So preparing for a second honeymoon with my second husband should have been—*what else?*—second nature to me. Or so I thought when he made the surprise announcement last month on our tenth wedding anniversary. I swooned like a schoolgirl as he detailed how we'd spend two glorious weeks together in France and Italy, where they practically invented romance. So what if we were well into the second half of our lives (unless, of course, we live to be 140), we were still young at heart, right? Right. But along with that lovely sentiment, allow me to offer a few tidbits I learned the hard way on our "second half" second honeymoon that may come in handy when planning yours.

1. Stay Young at Heart, but Pack (Both)Your Arch Supports

My feet began morphing into my mother's about ten years ago—bunions, fallen arches, planter fasciitis—and finding comfortable, somewhat fashionable shoes that accommodate my various orthotic devices has been my life's mission ever since. I felt like Cinderella the day I found a cute pair of black flats that were roomy enough to hold both my arch supports and my feet in reasonable comfort. I snapped them up and took them with me to Paris. Fast forward to the Champs-Élysées, where the pain in my left foot completely sidelined me after a very short stroll. Leaning against, appropriately enough, the *Arc de Triomphe*, I removed my shoes and saw the problem. Apparently, I'd gotten distracted when packing and had only put an arch support in the right shoe! So my very first purchase in the fashion capital of the world was a pair of Dr. Scholl's gel insoles at a pharmacy. So glamorous.

78

2. After a Certain Age, Jet Lag Is More Like Jet Sag

It had been a couple years since my last transatlantic flight, but I was fully prepared to have my circadian rhythm thrown off for a few days. I was not, however, prepared to have my jet lag express itself so conspicuously as upper eyelid sag. At my age, the only place I want to see droopy puppy dog eyes is on a puppy dog—and definitely not drooping back at me in the mirror. I swear that whole first week it would have taken a system of pulleys and levers to hoist my upper lids to an "awake" position. I took to hiding behind my sunglasses even when it wasn't sunny. Like inside, at night, in the shower.

3. There's Something Rotten in Venice, But It's Not the Canals

You know that god-awful smell that wet clothes take on when left sitting in the washer for two days? Well, that's the smell that accompanied us across Europe for two solid weeks during the hottest months of the year. The night before we left for our trip, I threw my default shoes, the white sneakers that allow me to walk pain-free for miles, into the washing machine and set them out to dry. The next morning they were a wee bit damp, so I wrapped them in a plastic bag and packed them. *Never Do This!* Unwrapping them when we hit Paris was like opening the Pandora's box of odors! Gagging on the noxious fumes, my husband and I raced each other to the nearest air vent. Since laundering the shoes in our hotel room was not an option, we tried to neutralize them with everything from expensive French perfume to medium-hold hair spray. The only thing that contained the stench was keeping my feet in the shoes, so I wore them—a lot. When I took them off, I had to wrap them in plastic and shove them in the farthest corner of the room so we could breathe freely. After one particularly sweaty day of walking in Venice, I had to hang them outside the bathroom window all night!

4. Fling Caution to the Wind, but Not Your Nightie.

Now let's face it, soaking up all the culture and history is fine and dandy, but this is a second honeymoon, dammit, so let's get down to the romance. Believe it or not, it is possible to still feel romantic post-menopause despite the unpleasant interference of stinky shoes, fallen arches and sagging eyelids. I'll leave to your imagination the maneuvers involved to accommodate one partner's bad knees and tennis elbow and the other partner's positional vertigo and carpal tunnel syndrome. What I want to warn you about is getting so caught up in the passion of the moment that your slinky new negligeegets flung across the bed and you completely forget about it until the next night when it's nowhere to be found—because it got wrapped up in the bed sheets and carted off to the bowels of the hotel laundry facility from which it will ne'er return. And you paid full price for it and everything!

So, there you have it, my friends. Learn from my mistakes and make your trip a smashing success. Of course, don't forget to take your sense of humor along with you, too. Trust me, you'll need it.

Happy (Second) Honeymooning!

30.
Karma and the Shame of Conducting Private Business in Public

I spent a good portion of my younger days pondering the central question of life: why am I here? Now in the full glory of post-menopausal wisdom, I can state unequivocally that I have been put on this Earth for two reasons, to humiliate myself and to eat crow. And, impressively enough, I recently accomplished both in one fell swoop.

My tale of karmic payback began some time ago when my mother was entering the twilight of her 96-year-long life. Though my sisters and I were obviously grateful she was still with us, she developed a habit that regularly had us crying out in frustration, "Why didn't you go before we left home?"

Without fail, the instant we crossed the threshold of any retail establishment, she declared her urgent—and previously nonexistent—need to use the bathroom. And for doing serious business, too; no "piddling" around for her. Her bowels beckoned with such maddening predictability on these excursions that my sisters and I were convinced she was somehow doing it on purpose to drive us crazy, much like her refusing to wear her hearing aids and then accusing us of whispering in front of her.

"Walking into a store is not a recognized intestinal trigger!" I vented in exasperation. *"It's not a thing!"*

To expedite the bathroom treks, my sisters and I memorized the layout of every nearby mall, shopping center and superstore with the diligence of thieves planning a heist. Even so, my mom could still throw us a curve ball, the most notorious of which became known as the gas station wino incident.

One afternoon an unexpected road closure landed us on a seedy stretch of highway with our gas tank edging close to "E." We kept our eyes peeled for a gas station among the mostly abandoned, graffiti-splattered buildings, and finally spotted a dilapidated but open one. My sister pulled into its littered lot. Our plan was to get in and out as fast as possible, pumping just enough gas to make it back to civilization. My mother's digestive system had other plans.

"I need to go," she announced decisively, insisting—over our loud protestations to the contrary—that this place didn't look so bad.

There was no reasoning with her, so in a desperate attempt to convince her of the unsuitability of this spot, my sister pulled around to the back of the building. She got out of the car and dramatically pulled open the rusted-through door to Exhibit A, thereby exposing the wretched wasteland of a bathroom, as well as taking the drunken vagrant lying in the middle of it—complete with a bottle in a paper bag—quite by surprise. (Despite his surprise, he was rather cordial, you know, in an E. coli carrier kind of way.)

We high-tailed it out of there and sped off down the highway, with my mother shouting the whole time about how we should have offered him some money to vacate so she could use the facilities. Seriously.

My mother has been gone more than four years now, and it turns out the joke is on me. In addition to some of her lovely qualities, it appears I have also inherited my mother's unattractive habit of "retail pooping," as I've indelicately come to call it. And despite what I formerly believed, it actually *is* a thing, according to Google. And I have it.

Name the store and I've probably used their facilities. From Target to Home Depot to El Corte Inglès in Madrid, I have made a beeline for the bathroom within minutes of entering. At first, I tried to pass it off as coincidence and my husband insisted it was psychological, but after the latest incident, I can no longer deny the force at work—it's karma, all right. Super-sized karma. With fries.

I was on my way home from work last week when I suddenly remembered that I needed candy for a class activity the next morning. I'd already passed the supermarket, so instead of backtracking, I decided to make a quick stop at a rather rundown Dollar Store up ahead. In the sixty seconds it took me to enter and walk to the candy aisle, the store worked its laxative magic on me with a magnitude too great to ignore.

Panicked, I ran to the back, praying a restroom would be there, while also mentally preparing myself for sanitary conditions several notches below a Walmart bathroom on Black Friday (which I'd actually once experienced). I whimpered in pain upon seeing the "Out of Order" sign on the women's room door. Directly across from it was the empty men's room, and my roiling intestines left me no choice but to duck in there. Fortunately, it was a single, but unfortunately, the lock was broken and the door was too far from the toilet for me to hold it shut with my hand or even my foot. So, there I sat, retail pooping in a rundown Dollar Store men's room, waiting for a wino to burst in on me and complete my humiliation.

They say your poor decisions, such as losing patience with your elderly mother, come back to bite you in the butt. Karma knew just where to find my butt, parked atop a Dollar Store toilet, and it surely put the bite on me. And I know my mom was laughing about it all the way from heaven.

31.
Going Batty

I am not a big fan of winged creatures, and I'm not much for the scurrying variety either. If a mad scientist ever combined the two into one hideous creation, say, some bizarre kind of a flying mouse—oh, wait, that's right, nature already *has*. It's called a bat and, despite my bat wing upper arms, I feel no affinity whatsoever with that creepy creature of the night.

I would have been quite happy limiting my lifetime bat exposure to the occasional late night bowl of Count Chocula, but Fate apparently had other plans for me. A few weeks ago I was staying with my daughter, who was eight months pregnant, to help with her toddler while her husband was out of town. The very first evening I arrived, I volunteered to do the laundry. I stopped just short of the door leading to the basement laundry room to give my daughter an impromptu shoulder rub in the hallway.

When she slowly drawled out, "M-o-o-o-m," I thought it was in appreciation of my superb massage skills. But less than a half-beat later, she cried, "What is that?"

I looked down at the black, spindly "fingers" inching out from under the door to the basement stairs. We both stood paralyzed for a second as the fingers became wings and then the wings spread to reveal a furry head.

Before we could even scream in terror, the flying mouse was swooping from one end of the kitchen to the other. It's possible we set a land speed record in fleeing to the safety of the guest room. With that door slammed securely behind us, the standard sit-com plot of "pandemonium ensues" became our reality, complete with panicked screaming, loud cursing and the spouting of wild solutions—including jumping out the window, calling an Uber and heading to a hotel. (We pretty much dismissed that idea out of hand since my granddaughter was asleep upstairs in her crib and it didn't seem right leaving her to fend for herself.)

As neither of us had a nuclear arms dealer on speed dial, my daughter called her husband who, despite having provided the likely point of entry for the bat by leaving the garage door open, failed to acknowledge the urgency of our situation. He refused, for example, to notify the National Guard on our behalf and instead instructed us in the official bat eviction protocol (which he later admitted he was making up on the spot). We were to turn off the all the inside lights, turn on the outside lights, open the doors and make noise, he explained.

"But we'll have to leave the guest room to do that!" I squealed, exposing the obvious flaw in his smarty-pants plan.

"Just remember that the bat is more afraid of you than you are of it," he replied.

"Not possible!" I screamed, as he was hanging up to return to the awards dinner he was attending.

My daughter put down her phone and transformed into a fierce bat warrior before my eyes. She, who was afraid of mushrooms as a child, put her hand firmly on the doorknob and announced we were going into battle. I attribute this sudden streak of courage in the face of flying rodents to the extra estrogen coursing through her veins. As a hormonally-starved, post-menopausal woman, I could hardly be expected to show the same level of bravery, which I believe accounts for my cowering behind her pregnant belly as she swung open the guest room door.

We spied our unwelcome guest circling the living room, so I dashed to open the front door as my daughter ran to handle the back. We then quickly repaired to the safety of the guest room, cracking the door open just wide enough to monitor the situation. After several mad passes around the dining room, the beast finally flew toward the open back door, but—and seriously, what are the odds here?—just as it was about to exit, a random gust of wind slammed the door shut. Curses!

Riding her estrogen and adrenaline high, my daughter bolted from the guest room, ran out the front door and around the house to prop open the back door. As she was coming back around, she said she felt something swoosh by overhead. Back at home base, we both waited with bated breath, hoping the absence of flapping sounds meant the visitor truly had gone.

We spent the next twenty minutes as bat-busters, cautiously opening closet doors and poking behind every piece of furniture with a broom to make sure no winged mammals were hiding anywhere. Then we jammed two beach towels in the space under the door to the basement to make sure nothing else could get through. When we were finally satisfied that we were alone, we headed to bed, physically and emotionally drained.

"Hey, Mom," my daughter called to me as she went up the stairs. "What about doing the laundry?

"I'm not opening the door to your basement again in my lifetime," I said. "Tomorrow, we'll find you a nice pick-up and delivery laundry service, my treat. And I won't so much as *bat* an eye at the cost."

32.
Forgive Me, George Clooney—A Love Not Meant to Be

Last week I traveled to Cincinnati, Ohio, to attend the 2018 National Society of Newspaper Columnists Conference. I always look forward to this annual gathering of the tribe, but this year's event in Cincinnati held a special attraction for me because someone I once believed would play a significant role in my life lived in the area and would be attending our group's luncheon. Years ago it seemed my future and his might be forever entwined, but, alas, our paths had diverged and we ended up in different worlds.

As I sat with my eyes fixed on the entrance to the dining room, a million fears flooded my mind. Would he be happy to see me? Would it be awkward? Would he wonder why I hadn't yet sprung for one of those Lifestyle Face Lifts? And then, suddenly, all my fears vanished because there he was, his presence filling the doorway, as handsome and imposing as I'd pictured.

I watched as he made his way through the eager crowd, easily chatting with folks along the way, confirming his charm was still fully intact. When he arrived at my table, my heart was nearly thumping out of my chest. I took a deep breath, rose to my feet and grabbed hold of the hand he extended to me. The veteran newsman and hometown hero certainly needed no introduction in this room, yet he smiled warmly and said, "Hello, I'm Nick Clooney. It's nice to see you here today."

"Hello, Mr. Clooney," I gushed. "My name is Lee Gaitan. It's such a pleasure to meet you, and, and..." I paused a moment before deciding it was best to be direct. "And you probably don't know this, but I was almost your daughter-in-law."

There, I'd said it. I'd addressed the elephant in the room. Well, the elephant in my head anyway. My "romance" with George Clooney may have been ancient news, but I felt his father had a right to know how bad I'd always felt for breaking George's heart, how much I wished it could have ended differently.

You see, back in the '90s George had pursued me shamelessly—right through my very own television screen in my very own living room—for two-and-a-half seasons of *ER*. Every Thursday night, there he was, blinking out Morse-coded messages to me with those soulful, bad-boy eyes. "Blink, blink, bliiiink," (I love you, Lee), "Blink, blink-blink, bliiiink," (I need you, Lee). Sometimes it was so blatant, it was embarrassing. Oh, I admit I whiled away many an afternoon daydreaming about a future with him, fantasizing about being part of the legendary Clooney clan. I even engaged in a little flirtatious blinking back. But I was married at the time and, as strongly as I was tempted, I ultimately changed the channel before we went too far to turn back.

George was crushed and became understandably gun shy about love afterwards. (I mean, look how long it took him to finally commit to marriage. Coincidence? I think not.) I'd always felt I owed the Clooney family an apology for the suffering I'd caused, and this was my chance to make things right. The essence of class, the elder Clooney graciously accepted my apology—*with a wink that could turn a steel girder to putty, by the way*—and even declined to alert security about me.

There was a bittersweet element to our goodbyes after the luncheon, with overly cheery promises to "stay in touch" that we both knew we'd never keep. I turned to look at him one more time as I was leaving the dining room. He was surrounded by admiring fans. To them, he was a distinguished broadcaster, an author, a political activist. But to me, he was, and will always remain, the road not taken. Nick Clooney—my former future father-in-law.

33.
Countdown to Disaster

Ladies and Gentlemen, I believe the disturbing experience I had today is proof positive that the Doomsday Clock is ticking toward the end of civilization as we know it.

I was in a hurry this morning and in a complete departure from my daily habit of at least 45 years, I neglected to put on my watch. Halfway to work, I started having that panicky feeling that I'd forgotten something. I quickly looked down to see if I was wearing pants—don't laugh, it happens. Fortunately, my pants were on (this time) and I was even wearing matching shoes, so I tried to dismiss the nagging thought that something was missing.

It was not until I was several minutes into teaching my "ESL for Millennials" class that I glanced at my wrist and made the shocking realization that it was buck naked, with only a faint tan line where my timepiece should have been.

"Yikes," I exclaimed. (Yes, I actually do use the word "yikes.") "I forgot to put on my watch. What time is it, you guys?"

And that's when the shock of forgetting my watch was completely eclipsed by my shock at seeing the entire class grab their phones to check the time. When I asked if anyone had a watch, I received only blank stares in response, as if I'd asked for a kerosene lamp. No one had a watch, not even a fancy high-tech one. I felt so old at that moment I thought I might sprout a dowager's hump on the spot.

I picked up my ear trumpet so I could clearly hear my class explain that watches are unnecessary nowadays when everyone has a phone. "We just look at our phones," they cried.

But, I countered, sometimes your phone isn't in front of you—it's in your purse, your pocket, your backpack, and it's inconvenient to get it out just to check the time.

Yes, they conceded, sometimes this was an issue. One student even lamented that it was indeed unfortunate you couldn't comfortably strap your phone onto your body (like, possibly on your wrist?), so you could steal a furtive glance at the time in a boring class—of course, not *my* class, he assured me.

Wow, a wearable clock, what a brilliant idea! If only someone would invent something like that. I thought my head would explode, but things were about to go even farther south. By sheer coincidence, part of the day's lesson involved making a timeline for daily activities. The students opened their books and pandemonium broke out when they came face to face with this horrifying sight.

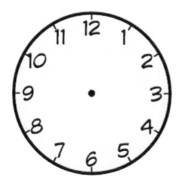

Yes, a blank clock face. Actually, several blank clock faces. The students were to draw hands on the clocks and write activities that corresponded to the times, using different verb tenses. For example, show the clock at 10:30 and write, "I had a meeting at 10:30 this morning."

"We don't know how to do that clock thing in English!" they all yelled out in panicked confusion.

In English? Now I was the one who was truly confused. Speaking English was not necessary to do that "clock thing," but it quickly became apparent English was not the issue. They had no clue how to draw hands on a clock or decipher what the big hand and the little hand signified when I did a few examples on the board for them. The stunning truth was they could only read digital clocks.

As I stood there, letting that realization sink in, I suddenly felt a bit faint and decided to dismiss class without even looking at anyone's phone. My stomach told me it was time for lunch and my husband was probably out in the parking lot, waiting to pick me up in our newfangled horseless carriage. I just prayed we made it home safely before the Doomsday Clock struck twelve.

34.
Surviving the Week before Spring Break

Today was the first official day of my spring break and it couldn't have come soon enough to please me. The week before a vacation always seems to drag, but this year the pre-break week was not only seemingly endless, but downright strange. Encountering a jumbo jet-sized palmetto bug in the middle of my bedroom in the predawn hours of Monday was my first clue that the week was not going to go my way.

If you are blessedly unfamiliar with this most loathsome of creatures, a palmetto bug is a giant flying cockroach that tends to live in palmetto (and other) trees, but is not above wandering indoors to terrorize law-abiding and highly insect-phobic citizens. Your run-of-the-mill indoor cockroach is a two-seater Cessna compared to the Airbus palmetto bug. They are huge, hideous and not at all what you want to plant your foot next to when rolling out of bed.

The worst part is, despite their gargantuan size, they are incredibly fast and able to squeeze through the smallest of nooks and crannies. Before I had a chance to grab a sizable weapon, the stinking thing skittered away and disappeared, I think, into a virtually invisible gap between the baseboard and carpeting in one corner of my bedroom. That meant, of course, it was just biding its time, waiting to ambush me at a later point. Try falling asleep with *that* image in your mind.

By Tuesday, I was so focused on the palmetto bug launching a surprise attack that I failed to see the dangerous obstacle that lay directly in my barefoot path to the kitchen. For some mysterious reason my dog Harper, whose mouth doubles as a Shop-Vac (seriously, he once tried to eat gravel and wood shavings to get to a fallen M&M), had uncharacteristically left sharp-edged Milk-Bone chunks uneaten on the kitchen floor. Stepping on a

Lego in your bare feet is nothing compared to impaling your instep on a Milk-Bone shard. New swear word combinations were needed to express the pain involved.

Wednesday I was afraid to get out of bed, but I managed to get dressed and off to work without a major mishap. I had planned a lesson for my class that involved the extensive use of that scourge of modern existence, technology. When I tried to log in to the computer in my room, I was "told" that I was an unrecognized user. Okay, I wasn't wearing mascara and my hair didn't look all that great, but seriously, I was unrecognizable? Just since the day before? Several log-in attempts followed, all with the same response. Fortunately, I had a backup lesson that could be presented by a living human being.

Thursday brought the kind of communication breakdown usually associated with Mercury in retrograde (which actually starts today, but maybe last week was a warm-up). At least this episode brought much needed comic relief to hell week. Some background info is required for this one. 1) My husband's first language is Spanish and he sometimes has trouble understanding English expressions. 2) My daughter, named Torrie, is very near her due date with baby #2. 3) Toys R Us is going out of business.

Those disparate facts led to a hilarious miscommunication between my husband and me Thursday evening. We were talking about the new baby coming when I suddenly remembered that Toys R Us was scheduled to start its liquidation sale soon. I grabbed my phone to check the store's website and saw that the sale was already underway. While looking at the screen, I exclaimed, "Oh, Toys R Us has started liquidating!"

My husband thought I was reading a text message, and I had said the words so fast that to him it sounded like *"Torrie's* started 'liquidating.'" He imagined "liquidating" might be an Americanism for her water breaking! We went back and forth several times, both completely lost in translation, with him not understanding why I wasn't more concerned about checking on my daughter, and me insisting I could buy whatever I wanted for the grandchildren without checking with her.

By Saturday, I was exhausted. I overslept and miscalculated the time I would need to walk the dog at the park and return home in time to change clothes for my hair appointment. After the walk, I had just enough time to drop the dog at home and continue straight to the hair salon. I surrendered my last bit of pride/shame and presented myself, covered in dog hair and muddy paw prints and without one drop of make-up on my post-menopausal face, to the perfectly coiffed, meticulously groomed receptionist. Although I've been going there for twenty years, I was afraid she might give me the same response my classroom computer had—unrecognized user.

Fortunately, she was more gracious. After squinting a little and turning her head sideways, she realized it was me and checked me in. Looking at my reflection in the mirror at the end of my appointment, I had to laugh. My stylist's usual expert job of coloring and cutting my hair was certainly at odds with the rest of my shabby appearance.

Well, I thought to myself, that old hairdresser joke is apparently true. It may be a *beauty* shop, darling, but they wield only curling irons, not magic wands.

Happy Spring Break!

35.
Early Warning System—Betrayal, Thy Name Is Bladder

When I was a little kid and violated the cut-off time for liquids before bed, my full bladder would often invade my dream, convincing me that I was already in the bathroom. The initial trickle of relief I felt was enough to wake me up and send me running to the bathroom for real.

Apparently, however, the post-menopausal years have pretty much disabled my bladder's early warning system. I learned this unfortunate fact a few weeks ago in possibly my most humiliating moment. I should have anticipated it, as I had been downright smug about my ability to "keep the door shut," unable to relate as my friends commiserated about cough drops, giggle drips and sneeze seepage. Despite osteopenia, insomnia and a few new bulges, I would always think to myself, at least I don't have leakage issues!

Well, pride goeth before a fall and I fell hard...into the deep, huge puddle formerly known as my mattress. I awoke that particular Saturday morning feeling really "sweaty." I kicked off the covers and felt around under me, slowly coming to the horrified realization that I was nearly swimming in a pond of my own making, and it wasn't perspiration. My nightgown was drenched to the waist, and the sheets, mattress pad and, worst of all, the down pillow under my knees were soaked as well. I jumped out of bed, ran to the linen closet and returned with an armload of bath towels to sop up as much of the rising tide as I could before it engulfed my sleeping husband.

How could this have happened, I wondered in total bewilderment, as I stripped off my wet nightgown to get in the shower. My trusty early warning system had broken down completely—no bathroom dream, no waking up, no nothing, just an ocean of processed Diet Coke and La Croix water! The sound of the shower woke my husband, who called out in confusion, "What's going on here?"

Shame-faced and wrapped in a towel, I stood before my husband and confessed what I'd done. And here's why my husband is truly a keeper. He shrugged, smiled and said, "Baby, this happens in the best of families." Then he helped me pull off all the bedclothes and put them in the washer. A little Lysol, Febreze and a good airing out with a fan took care of the damp spot on the mattress. Almost as good as new.

But I just couldn't leave well enough alone. When my husband went outside to cut the grass, I decided to try to rehabilitate the down pillow. Thinking of the many down jackets I'd washed over the years (and naively disregarding the feather differential there), I plopped the pillow into the washer. All was going well until the spin cycle. With a soaking-wet weight of approximately seventeen tons, the stupid pillow threw my washer so out of balance that the washer practically "womped" itself across the floor and out the door before I got to it.

I was ready to trash the pillow at that point, but my husband insisted he could wring it out in the bathtub. I envisioned this process entailing my stomping on it like Lucy in that famous grape-crushing scene, but he was actually able to get most of the water out without the use of my feet. So, I put my shoes back on and threw the pillow in the dryer with a couple tennis balls—just like you do with down jackets—and set the timer for the longest drying cycle.

When the dryer timer finally pinged, we anxiously pulled the door open, thereby unleashing a veritable explosion of goose feathers. There were feathers everywhere. Feathers upon feathers, flocks of feathers, I tell you, floating, swirling and spinning through the air. We had feathers in our hair, our ears and up our noses. We were choking on, coughing up and spitting out goose feathers for several minutes. What a mess my bird-brained bladder had created!

Now a few weeks post-disaster, we still encounter a feather or two here and there. In fact, just the other night, I was finishing up a project right before bedtime when I got a little thirsty. I opened the refrigerator and grabbed a can of La Croix. As I was about to pop the top, a little feather came floating down out of nowhere and landed on the can. I blew it off and promptly put the can back in the fridge.

Early warning message received. I have learned my lesson, my friends—a feather of prevention is worth a pillow of cure.

36.
An Alarming Adventure

The older you get, the greater your chances become of having to eat crow over something you misstated, misjudged or, as is typical for me, "mis-ridiculed" at an earlier point in your life. For example, it turns out that sensible shoes actually are the sensible choice once your aging arches are falling like London Bridge.

Having downed a crow's wing or two myself has made me sympathetic to others who find themselves with a plateful, but I admit I had to dig a little to find sympathy for my sister's avian meal the other day.

As the youngest in a family of tomboys, I was the odd one out, the girly-girl who played tea party instead of cops and robbers, who preferred ruffles to roughhousing. The only apparent concession I made to my male side was my total devotion to *The Three Stooges*, which my sisters ironically deemed offensive to their sensibilities. They spent their childhoods armed with cap guns, firing off round after round at imaginary bad guys, while a chunk of mine was spent in front of the TV, *nyuk, nyuk, nyuk-ing* it up with my boys.

"That nonsense is gonna rot your brain," they eye-rolled, their tone full of adolescent superiority. "A complete waste of time."

(Yeah, like those sulfur fumes from cap strips were brain food. And I'm learning plenty, I thought, as I rolled my eyes back at them.)

Fast forward more than a couple decades to the other night when my older sister was jolted out of a sound sleep by the blare of her smoke alarm. As she was desperately inspecting every inch of her house for smoke or flames, the alarm spontaneously stopped. After double-checking the house, she determined the alarm had simply malfunctioned. She crawled back into bed and had just drifted off when the blaring began again. She covered her ears and tried to wait it out, but after several minutes, the alarm was still going full blast.

She realized she'd have to disconnect it, but was very nervous about climbing up a stepladder with a bad knee that often goes out without warning. Not to mention, she'd witnessed my other sister lose her balance on a ladder, fall and break her hip. Out of ideas, she reluctantly dragged the ladder from of the garage and gingerly climbed up to reach the alarm. That's when she discovered that it was hardwired. So she climbed down, got a pair of scissors, climbed back up and snipped the wires. The alarm continued blaring in her hands. Apparently, she had some good back-up batteries, which, unfortunately, she couldn't figure out how to remove.

In frustration, she threw that devil's instrument out on the back patio and slammed the door shut. But it continued its god-awful blaring, so she retrieved it before the neighbors called 911. Turning back from the patio door, she spied her kitchen sink where she'd left a casserole dish soaking in soapy water and pitched the alarm into the water in a frantic attempt to drown the beast. She even turned on the hot water for good measure. Magically, the blaring started to die down and eventually stopped completely. She extracted the lifeless carcass from the sink and, with great satisfaction, tossed it in the trash.

I was dumbfounded. She had pretty much outlined a key scene from "Gents in a Jam," the Three Stooges episode in which they try a number of ways to turn off a radio that's playing an annoying song. Despite being unplugged, thrown out the window and stomped on, the radio will not "die" until Moe and Shemp finally drown it in the kitchen sink. "You got me...*glurg, glurgglurg*" are its final words.

"I don't know what made me throw it in the sink, but thank goodness I did," she said when she had finished recounting her harrowing adventure to me.

"Seriously?" I asked in disbelief. "You have The Three Stooges and me to thank for putting an end to your alarming nightmare," I explained, as I recounted the "Gents in a Jam" scene to her. "You obviously absorbed their lessons subconsciously. And to think you used to say watching them was a waste of time. Now excuse me while I go prepare your plate of crow."

"Well, I guess the last *nyuk, nyuk, nyuk* is on me," she chortled.

"Indeed it is," I sniffed. "And the last *caw, caw, caw* as well."

37.
Get the Bucket—Mom's Marriage Advice

My mom was a study in contrasts, a very sharp woman who quoted Shakespeare and Poe well into her 90s, yet whose declarations often smacked more of Yogi Berra. "You don't need to pay him," she once advised me when her neighbor changed my tire. "Just give him some money."

Any conversation with my mom could yield a bonanza of "Berra-isms." Years ago, suspecting she'd developed a blood clot in her leg, I rushed her to the ER, where the doctor confirmed my diagnosis and warned my mother away from the knee-high stockings she was sporting. "Absolutely the worst thing you can wear for circulation," he scolded.

"Oh, I don't actually wear them," she explained. "I just put them on."

When she was discharged a few hours later, she instructed me to pull the car up to the ER door and "beep the horn" for her. When I protested, insisting that blowing a car horn in a hospital zone was frowned upon, she replied, "No, of course, don't beep; just toot."

Along with unintentional humor, there was often a loopy kind of logic as well as a pearl of wisdom hiding within the shell of my mom's convoluted phrasing. I now know her explanation of menopause to be all too true. "It's like you become dumb for no apparent reason," she told my sisters and me.

But her marriage advice to my sisters and me was Mom at her most hilariously inscrutable best. "Sometimes," she counseled us, "you just have to get the bucket."

"What bucket?" we asked, utterly confused, but sensing a "Berra-ism" in the making.

"Well, say he's fixing something and he loses his patience, so he barks at you to bring him something he needs, like the bucket," she began. (For the record, that was a pretty accurate description of my dad's behavior when he got impatient with a project.)

"And you don't feel like being ordered around and getting the bucket," she continued. "Go in the bathroom and repeat just as mad as you want, 'I'm not getting him that *gee-dee*bucket' until you feel better. And then go get him the bucket."

When our howling over her head-scratching choice of a metaphor subsided, we all balked at what hit our liberated ears as advice to be submissive and stifle our feelings, so we dismissed it as another kooky Mom anecdote.

Now as a twice-married adult, I realize my mom was really saying that in marriage you have to give, bend and sometimes get the *gee-dee* bucket, even when you don't particularly want to. Sometimes practicing patience and biting your tongue—or venting your frustration in the bathroom, if necessary!—in the short run is the wisest choice in the long run.

It was the choice I myself made the other morning when I was awakened by my husband bellowing that our kitchen sink had sprung a sizable leak.

"Quick, get me the bucket!" he yelled urgently.

I leapt out of bed and hustled to the kitchen, bucket in hand. And I didn't even stop in the bathroom on the way.

As my husband and I mopped up the mess, I couldn't help thinking my mom was looking down from heaven, having a good chuckle at our expense. Pearls of wisdom? More like wisdom more precious than pearls. Thanks, Mom.

38.
The Perfect Storm—What the Winds of Fate Taught Me About Hope

Every now and then, the winds of fate blow in a curious pattern, sweeping up whatever is in their path and configuring it into a perfect storm of disaster. My perfect storm hit a few months back and included a baby, a runaway dog and a bowl of cat food. The mayhem that resulted put what I profess to believe to the test.

My daughter and her husband had left my two-month-old granddaughter in my care while they made a necessary out-of-town trip, and I was over the moon about getting to keep this little cupcake for a few days. I dropped her parents at the airport and, with my precious cargo aboard, carefully wended my way home through the nightmare of Atlanta's rush hour traffic. When at last I pulled into my driveway, safe and sound with a sleeping baby, I breathed a sigh of relief.

I thought I was playing it smart by parking in the wide-open space of the driveway instead of in the confined space of the garage where it would have been a tight squeeze to remove the car seat and take it into the house through the connecting door. So, I gently lifted the car seat to avoid disturbing the baby and headed to my front door instead. That's when the first unexpected gust of wind hit me in the face.

I had barely cracked the door open when my dog Harper, unhinged by my unusual entrance through the front door, bolted straight at me, nearly sending me (*and the baby*) crashing down on the sidewalk. Fortunately, I regained my balance before falling, but Harper, smelling freedom, was already a streak of brown, taking off down the hill. I bellowed after him, to no avail.

After I carried the car seat inside and set it safely down on the floor, I went back outside and ran around our cul-de-sac, yelling for Harper. Nothing. Harper has many good qualities, but coming when called is not one of them. Back inside the house, I grabbed my phone to text my husband at work. I wanted him to come home immediately and mount a search party.

As I reached for my phone, I suddenly remembered that in 10+ years of marriage, my husband had only forgotten to take his cell phone to work with him one time, today. With texting off the table, I punched in his office number instead. My husband is almost never at his desk, but I hoped this time would be an exception. Worse than no answer, I got a recording, informing me I had called a number that was not in service. Three more attempts with the same result proved I hadn't called the wrong number, but my calls would not go through. I felt the beginnings of a full-blown panic attack coming on. Every minute that passed likely took Harper farther away from home and, I feared, closer to the highway in front of our neighborhood.

As a last resort, I decided to email my husband, even though I knew without his phone on him, he'd likely not check his email until he was back at his computer at the end of the day. But with no carrier pigeons available, I was out of choices. I hit "send" and hoped the message would reach my husband in time. The email bounced right back to me with an error message that said his mailbox did not exist. What in the world was going on? I was sure any minute Rod Serling's voice would announce that I'd entered *The Twilight Zone*.

I took a deep breath and tried to regain my composure because I knew the baby had to be my top priority. As much as I love my Harper boy, there was no way I could leave the baby to go after him. "Well," I said aloud, "I'm always spouting off about the power of hope. I have no choice but to hold onto the hope that Harper will somehow be guided home safely."

By this time, the baby had begun to stir, so I lifted her out of the car seat and laid her on my bed to change her diaper. As soon as I got her diaper off, my doorbell rang. I answered the door, holding a half-naked baby, to find the sweet, gray-haired Korean man from a few doors down, pointing toward his house and trying to explain something to me in a mix of halting English and Korean. I only know how to say "hi" in Korean, so after "*Annyeong*" I was no help to him, but I thought I heard him say "dog."

Just then his teenaged grandson came running up and explained that Harper was in his grandfather's yard. I was so relieved I started saying "thank you" in every language I knew, although Korean didn't happen to be one of them. I grabbed Harper's leash and a Milk-Bone and handed them to the grandson.

"He'll come right to you if he sees a treat," I explained. "If you could put his leash on and bring him home, I would be so grateful. I'm here alone and can't leave the baby." (And you can't seem to dress her completely either, lady, they probably thought to themselves.)

The grandson relayed the plan to his grandfather and they headed back toward their house. I finally got the baby diapered—grateful that she hadn't leaked anywhere—and was marveling at how my hope had been rewarded. Somewhere in the midst of my marveling, I realized it was taking a very long time for my neighbors to return with Harper.

I wrapped a blanket around the baby and went outside to take a quick look down the street—just in time to see Harper dashing down the cross street, followed by the grandson waving a leash and a Milk-Bone in the air...and the grandfather, bringing up the rear, yelling something in Korean. Apparently, Harper had managed to elude their grasp.

I lost sight of the dog chasers, so I took the baby back inside the warm house, fed her a bottle and held onto my hope for Harper's safe return. About ten minutes later, grandfather and grandson again knocked at my door, this time with the wayward Harper in tow. They'd found him at the end of the street in another neighbor's open garage, chowing down on a bowl of cat food. Harper may love to run like the wind, but not as much as he loves to eat. And why settle for one crummy Milk-Bone when the smell of tuna is in the air?

The grandson told me that after he'd attached the leash, Harper insisted on finishing the entire bowl of free food before allowing himself to be led out of the garage. The instant I opened my door, Harper charged into the house as wildly as he'd charged out of it, except now he was covered in wet mud, which he generously spread all over the carpets I'd spent $150 to have cleaned exactly one week before.

All three of us now exhausted, and at least two of us with full bellies, we collapsed, me in the rocker with babe in arms and Harper on the floor at my feet. The winds were calm; the storm had passed. The rhythmic breathing of contented infant and canine slumber was the only sound. I snuggled the baby close to me, rubbed Harper's head with my foot and shot a grateful glance heavenward.

Emily Dickinson wrote that hope is the thing with feathers, but my perfect storm taught me that hope rewarded is the thing covered in muddy brown fur. And, P.S., sometimes hope waves a Milk-Bone and speaks Korean.

Bonus Tracks From the Vault

This year marks twenty years since the publication of my first book, **Falling Flesh Just Ahead…and other signs on the road to midlife**. (If I wrote that book now, I'd have to change the title to FALLEN Flesh.) In honor of that anniversary, and the complete loss of even the illusion of my youth, please enjoy these four bonus chapters from that book!

39.
I May Break, but I Will Not Blend

I used to get so mad at my father when I was growing up because he could make an entire year of holidays vanish in the blink of an eye. "So, today's the last day of school," he'd say to me every June. "Well, pretty soon it'll be the Fourth of July, then Labor Day, and before you know it, you're back in school. Thanksgiving and Christmas are come and gone and, that's it, another year is finished." I thought he was crazy. Anyone with any sense at all knew that summer vacation lasted forever and Christmas never came soon enough

Then sometime in my thirties, I noticed that holidays were occurring at closer intervals. It was subtle at first, a minor Halloween/Thanksgiving decoration overlap (same basic colors, so I wasn't overly concerned). When I had to take the pine boughs off the mantle to make room for the Easter eggs, I blamed the federal government. "Darn those Monday holidays, they've thrown off my entire schedule!" This year I actually sent my goddaughter a package in February to simultaneously mark her past September's birthday, Christmas, and Valentine's Day. "Happy Birthmastine's Day!" I exclaimed cheerily, vainly attempting to cover my horror at having misplaced nearly six months of my life somewhere.

But that's how aging works. It doesn't have the guts to walk up and look you in the face; it sneaks up in small, insidious ways. Aging insinuates its way into your life with empty promises. "Think how much time and trouble you can save by celebrating three occasions at once," it coos, appealing to your time-starved sensibilities. Holidays that once had distinct, unique identities are lumped together in one nondescript, but ever-so-efficient, "Birthmastine's Day." You don't realize until it's too late that the relatively benign blending of holidays is only a short step away from the most pernicious blending of all, the blending of your very self. Blending just like Nancy Casey, a.k.a., the gray lady.

Nancy Casey was an accountant at a public relations agency where I once worked. Her main function in life was to issue purchase orders while wearing gray. She wore gray so long and hard that her hair and then her skin turned gray—of course, her personality had a jump start on all of this, being without color since the foundation of the world—and then she just simply *was* gray. It was awful because the walls and carpeting of our offices were—you guessed it, gray—and no one could ever tell if Nancy was in her office or not because she blended right in. You just had to stand there talking into this large expanse of gray nothingness, waiting for a voice to respond, "Do you have backup for all of these purchases?" Nancy Casey blended.

Blending is one of my greatest fears, surpassing even my long-standing fears of the metric system and Silly Putty. (When I was young my sister told me Silly Putty could come out of its shell unprovoked and attach itself to my body in hideous ways, which accounts for the fact that I have slept with one eye open ever since.) Centimeters, plastic eggs, and blending—these are the things that go bump in my night.

Lately, however, the blending question has become more than an academic concern. I have reason to believe that the process may have started. I might as well come clean: I failed to engage people at a recent dinner party. People counted on me, and I let them down. I was dull. I was drab. I was bored out of my mind. And I didn't even try to hide it. Yes, these were tiresome people, people who would have to study for a personality test, but that is all the more reason why I was needed. I should have rallied and feigned interest. I am, after all, a world-class feigner. I am a professional, for crying out loud. I can convince people they are having fun while undergoing, or at least while performing, root canal surgery. After completing three back-to-back root canals on me, my endodontist, weak with laughter, told me that was the most fun she'd ever had in rubber gloves. (That meant a lot to me, considering she is a dentist and not a proctologist.)

In the past twenty years, I can think of only one time when I was less charming than I was at this party. But even then, as soon as the last stitch of the episiotomy was pulled tight, I regained my sparkling sense of humor. The obstetrician commented that I was "most pleasant". . . when I wasn't screaming to have his head served on a platter, that is. Actually, I believe I was demanding to have his head served on a (insert a very bad word here) platter, but you get the idea.

But all of that is in the past. Let's face it, now I'm blending. Just like Nancy Casey. "You are exaggerating. You are not blending!" my sister insists. Oh, really? Then what does account for my lackluster performance at that party? The barometric pressure? Something I ate? Hey, wait one gray, blended minute. I did have a near toxic level of aspartame in my bloodstream that night, which could conceivably cause aberrant behavior. Work with me; it's possible. Remember the famous Twinkie defense? Why not the Twinkie Light defense?

After many sleepless nights (and fruitless inquiries into the aspartame industry), I decided there was nothing to do but confront the blending issue directly. I called a woman who was at the party and asked her straight out if she had noticed anything strange about my behavior that night. "At the party?" she asked distantly. "Gosh, were you there? That's funny, I don't remember seeing you."

Was I there? Doesn't remember seeing me? Was this definitive proof of blending or what? It was too horrible. I had to lie down in a darkened room and remain very still for several hours after I hung up the phone. And it was a good thing I did, too, because it turns out I'm going to need all my strength. I just realized that

Birthmastine's Day is right around the corner, and I haven't even started my shopping yet!

40.

For Sale by Owner: Slightly Used Skylight, Two-by-Fours Optional

The desperation of aging makes you do crazy things. Like asking your older sister for advice. I was going to ask my older sister Sam if she thought I should color my hair. Then I remembered she was the same sister who convinced me to "do something" about my caterpillar-like eyebrows when I was in tenth grade. As the anointed beauty guru of our family—she had been to New York City on at least two separate occasions—her ruling was immutable. "Something must be done," she said decisively, "and I'm the one to do it." I nodded in agreement, unwittingly giving her permission to commit what can only be classified as a hate crime against my face.

Dismissing the tweezers as inadequate for the mammoth task before her, she snatched up a razor with a brand-new blade and began shaving my unruly eyebrows into submission. Yes, I said shaving. A moment of silence, please. The result was not exactly the graceful arch I had pictured. The words, "burn victim" don't begin to describe it. Browless, I went to school. Browless, I went to church. Browless,I lived, and browless, I was certain, I would die—of acute embarrassment. When my other sister Eileen saw me, she bowed her head and said three Hail Marys for the repose of my soul, certain that death by public humiliation was very near. It was a tenth-grade nightmare beyond all imagination. Not even Bill Clinton could have felt my pain.

Still, watching the gray hairs on my thirty-nine-year-old head multiply faster than rabbits was enough to make me consider giving Sam another chance. Shoot, I reasoned, in the years since the Great Shave-Off Sam had actually lived in New York City for extended periods of time. Besides, it had been at least a year since I'd had my last revenge dream about her. (The one where she's held down by a large woman named Hilda and given a bikini wax without sedation.) I had nothing to lose but my gray, I decided. As I reached for the phone, it rang. When I picked it up, I heard Sam's voice at the other end. It was fate, confirming my renewed faith in my sister.

"You must come over at once!" she blurted. The desperation was unmistakable.

"What's wrong?" I asked in panic.

"It's fallen off." She choked out the words between deep sobs.

"What? What has fallen?" I asked urgently.

"The house. . . the light. . . completely fallen off," she mumbled, nearly incoherent.

Sam had just moved to a newly built house, and I had visions of roofs collapsing and walls sinking into the ground. "Tell me what has fallen," I instructed her, using the same measured tone that those "Rescue 911" operators employ when delivering babies over the phone. "Just fallen, fallen completely off." It was futile to try to get an answer out of her when she was like this. I left for her house immediately.

I braced myself for the devastation I would witness when I arrived at the house, but as I pulled up in the driveway, everything looked intact. Must be an interior wall, I thought. The door was open so I went in, calling to my sister as I wandered from room to undevastated room. Everything looked fine, but Sam was nowhere to be found. Finally, I heard some whimpering coming from upstairs and followed it, expecting to find one of the cats mewing in protest at its new surroundings. Instead, the trail of sighs led me to Sam's bedroom, where I found her slumped down in the corner, her face buried in her hands.

"What's going on?" I asked in confusion.

"I didn't really think it would happen to me. But it's fallen," she said.

"What has fallen?" I demanded impatiently.

"This!" she said, lifting her head. "My face. It has fallen totally off."

"Oh, is that all?" I asked, relieved. "I thought it was your roof trusses or your floor joists."

She was unmoved by my knowledge of construction terms.

"It's my own fault," she continued. "What is a woman my age doing building a house with all these windows? 'I want a house that's flooded with light,' I said. 'I want a skylight over my vanity,' I said. What was I thinking? This," she said, pointing to her face, "is what a skylight over your vanity gets you—a fallen face."

"Your face hasn't fallen," I said.

"You're just humoring me, "she said. "Look me in the eye and say that," she challenged.

I cupped both her chins in my hand, looked into her eyes and said solemnly, "Your face has not fallen."

"No?" she ventured cautiously.

"No," I said. I paused for a moment before adding, "Okay, it has maybe 'slidden.' But just a little." This was as close as I might ever get to eyebrow payback, and I was going to make the most of it.

"Don't toy with me," she pleaded. "This is not 'slidden' face," she said, pinching a fold of flesh from under her chin. "This is fallen face."

"That," I said, "is not face at all. That is another anatomical structure entirely."

"What is it?"

"You don't want to know," I told her.

"Yes, I do. I have to know. You have to tell me," she said, near tears.

"Okay, but it's not pretty," I said, feeling a bit flushed with the power I suddenly held over her. I could almost feel my eyebrows growing thick. "That's wattle."

"Wattle?" she asked, confused.

"Yes, wattle," I replied, "A fleshy, wrinkled fold of skin hanging from the neck or throat, characteristic of chickens, turkeys, some lizards, and, in your case, certain women over forty."

"I'm going to vomit now," she said calmly, closing her eyes.

"Although, to be precise, you do not actually have wattle," I continued authoritatively.

"I don't?" she asked hopefully.

"No, you have what is termed 'incipient wattle.' Of course, incipient wattle inevitably progresses to full-blown wattle," I explained.

"How much time do I have," she asked.

"Well, don't be shocked if next Thanksgiving you feel an uncontrollable urge to crawl onto the serving platter and surround yourself with cranberries. If you catch my drift."

She cringed. This was fun.

"In other words, incipient wattle today, pin feathers tomorrow. I'll be gobbling by the end of next week," she said with grim resignation.

I couldn't stand it any longer. I burst out laughing. "Oh, get a grip," I said. Your face has not fallen, and you do not have wattle, incipient or otherwise."

"Really?" she asked.

"Really," I told her. "But you are right about one thing. There is entirely too much light in this bedroom. My hair looks like Nancy Casey's in this light. In fact, I wanted to ask you—

"As in Nancy Casey, the gray lady?" Sam gasped, horrified. "Well, that does it," she added definitively. "I'm selling this house. How many women's illusions of youth must be destroyed before I take action?"

"Isn't that kind of extreme?" I asked. "Let's call Eileen and see what she thinks. She lives in Florida, a state known for bright sunlight. She must have developed some coping skills."

"True," Sam agreed. "Plus, she's even older than we are."

We called our older sister, who assured us via speakerphone that, based on her years of experience with unforgiving sunlight, selling Sam's house was unnecessary. "Which is not to say that it doesn't need some alterations," she explained. "First, hang fully lined hotel/motel-type window coverings on every pane of glass in the house. Next, put low-wattage bulbs in all the light fixtures and drape gauze over all lamps. And most important," Eileen added emphatically, "board up every last skylight. Climb out on the roof with a load of two-by-fours yourself if you have to, but cover them. Believe me, it's the only way."

She was beyond brilliant.

"You do realize that the actual appearance of your face will not change, but your perception of it will. At our age, that's worth a lot," she concluded.

"And will this work for my hair as well?" I asked.

"What's wrong with your hair?" Eileen asked.

"It's really looking gray, especially in this light. I thought maybe I should do something with it."

Sam seemed to perk up at the sound of these words. "Do something with it," she repeated.

"Yeah, highlight or color it. What do you think?"

"Hmm," said Eileen as she mulled over this possibility.

Suddenly, I caught Sam's reflection in the mirror. She was more animated than she had been all day. She looked positively energized. What is going on, I wondered.

"No, you don't want to highlight or color it," said Sam, walking toward me with her hand behind her back. Was that a gleam in her eye?

Instinctively, I started backing away. "I don't?" I asked.

"No," she said, moving closer to me. "Why bother with all that mess when it's so much simpler to . . . shave it off!" She whipped a razor out from behind her back and thrust it high in the air above my head. "It'll be such a good look for you. You don't have to shave all of it, just the gray parts." She was poised to strike when I shrieked, "No! Not this time, you New York City dropout, you beauty guru imposter. I'm out of here."

"What's going on there?" Eileen screamed.

"She's got a razor, Eileen, and she's not afraid to use it," I said breathlessly.

"Run, Lee, run," shouted Eileen.

"That's what I'm doing," I called as I made a beeline for the door. Charging down the hall, the razor-wielding Sam in hot pursuit, I could hear the disembodied voice of Eileen on the abandoned speaker phone back in the bedroom.

"Hail Mary, full of grace," she intoned, "the Lord is with thee. . .

If you ever think fate is calling you on the phone, hang up!

41.
Burned by the Flame of Youth

Of all the rituals women employ to stave off the debilitating effects of aging, surely the total facial makeover remains one of the most time-honored and humiliating. My friend Kate read that world-renowned makeup artist Anthony Roberts was coming to Atlanta and for a mere fifty dollars would be only too happy to laugh in your face and say things like, "Oh, my dear, someone apparently ignored your instructions not to be resuscitated." Kate was steamed about her husband's spending so much money on golf and wanted to frivolously waste some herself to even the score.

"Hmm, let me get this straight," I said. "You're mad at your husband, so it's going to cost me fifty dollars?"

"Exactly. Now get ready because our appointments are for ten this morning."

"Are you crazy? I can't be ready by ten. It'll take me two hours just to do my makeup and hair," I said. "Plus, I have to find something stylish to wear."

"It's a makeover. Who cares what you look like going in?" Kate said. "They can't take our 'before' pictures without our permission. Lurlene said so."

"Who the heck is Lurlene?" I asked

"She's the young cosmetics woman at Macy's, and she's ever so earnest," Kate replied. "Her exact words to me, as she gazed sincerely into my eyes were, 'Oh, no, ma'am, I don't believe they'd dare do that with you.' What exactly do you think she meant by that? Well, in any case, Lurlene would not lie."

"I'm glad you and Lurlene have bonded so beautifully," I said, "but you just don't get it, do you?"

"Get what?"

"You're not going to wear any makeup to a makeover?"

"Well, no, I'm not."

"Have you lost your mind? That's like saying you aren't going to clean your house before the cleaning lady comes. You wouldn't dream of doing that, would you?" I asked

"Well, of course not," Kate answered impatiently. "Do you think I want her to know what a slob I really am?"

"Then why would you expose your naked face to public ridicule and scorn? Listen to me, you greenhorn. Makeovers are no place for amateurs. Lurlene's ostensible earnestness aside, Mr. Anthony Roberts has one goal in mind: to indict us on charges of criminal ugliness, no matter how good we look in our 'before' pictures, so that we can buy our freedom with his beauty products. If you go in there naked-faced, you will be convicted before you can say 'alphahydroxy.' By the time he's through sentencing you, there won't be an eye pencil left unsharpened in the state of Georgia. Your Visa card, not to mention your ego, will never recover."

"Oh, you're right. I don't know what I was thinking," she said. "It's just that Lurlene seemed so innocent, so believable— hey—you don't think Lurlene was in on it, do you?" Kate asked.

"I'm not saying that," I replied. "Certainly, I've seen that scam before, but she could just as easily be a pawn in their dirty little game. It's possible she's in over her head."

"Oh, that poor girl," Kate sighed. "The makeover business is nasty."

"Indeed it is," I said knowingly, and we set about putting our best face forward.

The truth is, I didn't have all that much experience with pricey in-salon makeovers myself—enduring in-kitchen Mary Kay makeovers had been more my unfortunate experience—but I had a pretty good idea of how they worked. I knew these people preyed shamelessly on women's insecurities for profit. I imagined it would go something like this: A woman tentatively approaches the appointment desk, eyes downcast, "Do you think Mr. Roberts would see me next week? I know it's a lot to ask, with my T-zone having such irregular borders and all —it's a temporary hormonal problem I'm having—but I'm willing to pay extra." Her request is discreetly handled by a non-threatening Lurlene-type who makes her feel safe and convinces her to let down her guard. Once the poor woman actually says the words, "Oh, this is going to be fun," they know they've got her! The unsuspecting woman then shows up, naively naked-faced, at the appointed hour, expecting to be warmly greeted by her confidante Lurlene—who, by the way, graciously assured the woman earlier that her irregular T-zone, while obviously problematic, would be handled with the utmost professionalism. To her great shock, she is promptly handed over to a cadre of severely made-up women, dressed from head to toe in faux Left Bank black. By the time she is led into the inner sanctum to see the great and powerful Oz, she is too intimidated to ask why she needs three different toners and four different replenishers when she only has one face. (Just as she could never admit to her hair stylist that she has trimmed her own bangs between cuts. "The ends just started breaking off," she'll say. "It was really weird.") No, her only thought at this point is getting her credit limit upped so that she can begin to make amends for every untightened pore on her unclarified face.

Well, Kate and I would not be led as sheep to the slaughter. We were going in prepared!

"Mr. Roberts will see you now," said the surprisingly—and, I thought, deceptively—friendly handmaiden. As steeled as I was for this experience, the words still struck terror in my heart.

Kate and I were ushered in separately—of course, divide and conquer—but I was determined not to crumble. I was presented to Mr. Roberts, an imposing patrician-looking man with a silver mane. He said nothing as he surveyed me up and down, clipboard in hand. I coughed nervously. I can't let him get to me, I thought. His eyes darted in staccato movements from my hair to my nails to my probably ill-chosen hosiery. After a few moments of silence, he spoke. "And this is your look?" he asked.

"Yes, this is it. Pretty much. Mr. Roberts, sir," I answered, feeling my chest tighten.

A hint of derision quivered at the corners of his mouth. "Yes, of course, it would be," he sniffed and began marking up the form on his clipboard, finishing each notation with a great flourish.

More nerve-wracking silence followed as he scribbled away on his clipboard. Why didn't I wear the black dress, I scolded myself. It's so much more sophisticated. And lip liner, I can't believe I forgot lip liner. Oh great, I thought, any minute now a fashion police S.W.A.T. team is going to rush the place and take me down. My rap sheet will identify me as Lee "Démodé" Potts. Just as I was about to ask for my one phone call, Mr. Roberts began firing questions at me. "What is your blood type? Do you have a history of fainting? Are you allergic to anesthesia?" Routine beauty questions.

He paused dramatically after I finished answering, then turned, looked at me eye to eye and asked purposefully, "Would you wear red lipstick?"

"Yes?" I replied, somewhat unsure of what the correct answer was.

"Tell me again," he demanded. "Would you really wear it?"

"Yes, I would," I said more strongly. "I would definitely wear it."

"But you must convince me that you would not simply wear it, but *wear* it, inhabit it, color your life with it, or I shall not waste my time prescribing it for you."

"Oh, but I would wear it," I pleaded, the need for red lipstick suddenly becoming even more urgent than the need for my own personal salt lick on days twenty-one through twenty-seven of my cycle. "Indeed, I would do more than wear it, or inhabit it, I would become it. My heart, my soul, my very essence would be red lipstick, now and for all eternity. Please, please, you must prescribe it for me. I will prove myself worthy,"

"Very well then. I'm going to take a chance on you," he answered and dispatched one of the handmaidens to the vault to fetch a thirty-dollar tube of Flame Eternale, my soul's new essence in an emollient-rich base. I felt so blessed.

The actual reconstruction of my face passed in a blur. I was giddy with delight after Mr. Roberts pronounced my skin, eyes and lips to be "definitely not awful." Imagine, he said that! About me, a commoner! Of course, he had to take points off for my having eyebrows that looked like "two unfinished sentences," but that was only fair. (I thought it was wise to keep mum about the Great Shave-Off.)

The makeover turned into a virtual lovefest, with the handmaidens fawning over me, Mr. Roberts hovering nearby to ensure the proper foundation coverage, and everyone showering compliments on me. (Mr. Roberts' compliments were a bit tricky to decipher, though, couched as they were in pompous affectation.) Didn't I tire of people telling me how beautiful I was, the handmaidens wanted to know. (Actually, I have nearly unlimited stamina in that area.) Didn't I drive men absolutely wild with my incredible eyes, they asked repeatedly. (No, but some have gotten pretty worked up over my homemade stuffed peppers.) Oh, how could I have been so wrong about these people? They were committed to my welfare, to helping me unleash the beauty that lay dormant inside of me, the beauty that Flame Eternale would now set ablaze forevermore.

When at last I was allowed to rejoin Kate, we both stood and stared at each other's transformation. I spoke first. "I am Flame Eternale," I said.

"And I, "she said momentously, "I am Tulipe Mystique."

The intensity of the moment gave both of us goose bumps. We couldn't buy our forty-seven different "prescriptions" fast enough, although I skipped all the skin-care items and doubled up on the glamour products, preferring style over substance any day.

"Who would have thought happiness like this could be had for a mere three hundred dollars, plus tax?" I marveled.

"And to think you said they would try to take advantage of us," Kate said. "Intimidate us into buying lots of useless cosmetics. Everyone was so nice."

"I know. I never felt any pressure from anyone. I mean, I practically had to beg Mr. Roberts to let me get the Flame Eternale. I was really wrong about this."

"You sure were," Kate laughed. "But, then again, they could tell they weren't dealing with a couple of pikers, either."

"Yeah, that's for sure." I added in agreement.

And so we two savvy women went on our merry way, proving once again that shameless flattery outsells sneering degradation every time.

42.
They're Ba-ack

Eighteen years ago a friend and I accidentally went out on a date with two convicted criminals named Mike and Tony. Oh, grow up, it happens. (Of course, pray to God it never happens to you.) I tell you this now because I have recently learned a painful lesson: The older you get, the greater the chances that a dreadful incident from your past will return to haunt you. Mushroom farmers-cum-drug-dealers-cum-entrepreneurs, Mike and Tony defy easy description. In fact, an incomplete description of Tony (or "Tone," as he is affectionately known) is what led to my regrettable decision to be the "fourth" on that fateful night so many years ago.

It was the summer after our senior year in college, and my friend and I were housesitting for her vacationing parents. We were determined to pack in as much adventure as possible before real life, complete with real jobs, began in September. This is a daunting task in a town of about three thousand, but like most know-it-all twenty-one-year-olds, we welcomed the challenge.

We were sound asleep one morning when the phone, blaring like an air-raid siren on steroids, abruptly woke us at the ungodly hour of eleven A.M. (We'd only crawled into bed a few hours earlier.) Ginny answered it, and I heard her mumbling in agreement that last night had been "pretty wild." I was struggling to recall if I had been any part of that wildness when I heard her straightforward, but polite rebuff: "Thanks for the offer, but, see, we generally don't get 'wasted' before noon . . . and, well, we don't ever do *that*, either before or after noon."

My mind was racing. Well, as much as it could on three hours of sleep. Who was this person? My memories of the previous night were somewhat patchy. I remembered that this cute guy I'd had a crush on a few summers before had asked me out and had driven Ginny and me to the party. I remembered dancing very closely with my cute guy somewhere between my second and third rum and Coke (which was about two and a half more than I usually had or could handle). I remembered thinking that you could pass out at this party and never fall down because there were so many people packed into the room. I remembered my shoe falling off at one point and being utterly stymied about how to put it back on. (Perhaps this was between the fifth and sixth rum and Coke?) I remembered thanking my cute guy profusely for so brilliantly cracking the shoe code—he effortlessly slipped it back on my foot as if he'd been doing it all his life—as well as for agreeing not to drink so he could drive me home.

But, try as I might, I couldn't remember meeting anyone who would call and propose untoward activities at eleven o'clock in the morning. Just then Ginny said, "Well, yes, we do eat and swim, but again, not before noon." I was right in her face at this point, demanding to know who it was. She covered the phone with her hand and whispered, "It's Mike. From last night. He's asking if we want to go swimming or out to eat."

"Who? I asked again, still confused.

"Oh, that's just Lee," Ginny said into the receiver. "She's staying with me. Well, I don't know, I'd have to ask her. What's your cousin's name? What does he look like?"

I began wildly gesticulating my disapproval for the emerging plan.

"Look," said Ginny to Mike. "We'll talk it over and call you back in a little while."

"Who is this Mike person and did we make him any promises we have no intention of keeping?" I asked, vowing never to even drink Coke again, much less Coke with rum in it.

"No, it's just Mike. You know, Mike from last night," she replied matter-of-factly.

I shook my head "no."

"Remember I came over and told you I smelled someone wearing Polo? Well, I followed the trail, and it ended at Mike."

"You smelled him at a party, so now I have to go out with his cousin?" I asked.

"Lee, it was Polo," she said with finality.

Unfortunately, I completely understood the insane allure of Polo. Several months earlier I had tracked a middle-aged, moderately unattractive gentleman through the entire Kmart shoe department on Christmas Eve just to get a whiff. What was supposed to be a quick stop to load up on AAA batteries turned into a forty-five-minute discount store safari.

"Do I at least get to know his name?" I asked with resignation.

"His name is Tony, and Mike says he's really funny," she said a little too enthusiastically.

We decided on the dinner option because I was not putting on a bathing suit for someone I didn't know, and Ginny, who had stopped shaving her legs earlier in the summer as a political statement, was determined not to compromise her beliefs—even for Polo. Seven P.M. came, and my heart was pounding. We saw their car pull up in front of Ginny's house. A tasteful dark-blue Saab. So far, so good. (Like axe murderers can't drive Saabs.) I saw Mike get out. He was relatively decent looking. Tall, kind of lanky, dirty blond hair, wearing jeans and a cotton sweater. Okay, some dermabrasion wouldn't have hurt, but he appeared normal enough. And then I saw my mystery date, Tone, as he unfolded himself from the passenger seat. All 250 pounds of him. Remember the fat Elvis stamp that everyone rejected?

Remember Nick Tortelli, Carla's ex-husband on "Cheers"? If the two of them had a love child, it would be Tone.

The closer they got to the front door, the louder my whimpering got. Ginny opened the door, and I was face to face with the largest swatch of polyester I'd ever seen in my life. (And I had seen *Saturday Night Fever* six times.) Tone was an absolute vision in Quiana. There was not a natural fiber to be found on him, unless, of course, you counted body hair, which was a different story altogether.

And what a conversationalist. "Hi, I'm, like, Tony, heh-heh, but everyone calls me, like, Tone and that. I don't know why, heh-heh. It's, like, funny, you know? Heh-heh." Oh, yeah, Tone, it's, like, downright hilarious. Tone and I sat in the backseat of the car, where I plastered myself against the door. I figured falling out on a sharp turn couldn't be any worse than what I was already enduring. And there were a lot of sharp turns on this mountain road leading to the restaurant. I thought Mike was taking them hard on purpose to launch me across the seat into Tone's Quiana-draped arms. In between thinking up painful ways for Ginny to die, I made a few stabs at conversation.

"So, Tone, what do you do?" I asked.

"I'm, like, into mushrooms and that," he said.

"You mean eating them . . . and that?" I continued.

"No, growing them," he replied, setting me straight. "Hey, that was kind of a joke you made, huh? Heh-heh, you're, like, funny and that," he marveled.

"And that," I nodded.

It turns out old Tone was a sort of mushroom magnate, having descended from one of the most influential mushroom farm families in the tri-county area. Heck, he was practically royalty, having been crowned king of the Fungus Festival for two years running. Our fascinating conversation was interrupted when Mike took what was clearly a 25-mph turn at seventy-five. Ginny and I both gulped loudly. Mike apologized and said he was still getting used to driving this car.

"Oh, did you just get it?" I asked.

"No, it's Tone's," he said.

"And he makes you drive him around because he's the mushroom king?

"Not exactly," said Mike. "He's not allowed to drive yet. See, I got out first.

"Of the military?" Ginny asked.

"Of prison, actually," replied Mike, careening around yet another turn in the road.

"Yeah, but we did wear uniforms and that," Tone, the quipster, quickly added.

I am a person who cannot stand awkward silences even when they are preferable to awkward conversation, so I jumped right in with, "Let me guess, the charge was vehicular homicide."

"Reduced to involuntary manslaughter. That vehicular homicide charge was so bogus," Mike explained, as he slammed on the brakes to avoid rear-ending the car ahead of us.

We finally did find out that Mike and Tone, those wacky guys, were just kidding about the nature of the charges. True, they had been nabbed for a moving violation, but it was the controlled substances the police found in their car that caused the real problem. And in a show of great cousinly solidarity, Tone said he was driving–even though it was really Mike–because with Mike's previous driving record, his license would have been permanently revoked on the spot. Tone took the rap, man. A condition of his parole was that he not operate a moving vehicle for six months.

"So, we never really killed anybody or anything," Tone laughed. I felt so reassured that I decided to let Ginny arrange all my dates for me from then on. After all, I'd never found anyone of Tone's caliber on my own, had I? The rest of the date included the following highlights:

> 1) A stop at a poorly lit bar that Ginny and I had heard had developed a shady reputationin recent years. Mike and Tone insisted they had never been there before, but when we walked in, the bartender, a short, elderly gentleman standing ona stool, yelled across the room, "Hey, Mr. Mike, Mr. Tony, the usual?" Mike mumbled something about cutting the legs off his stool before we left.

> 2) Mike's suggestion that we go to an even shadier establishment to see a strip show performed by a sixty-year-old woman with a football-shaped surgical scar on her abdomen. It was not easy talking him out of that.

> 3) My pretending to be unconscious on the way home so Tone would leave me alone. When Tone asked, "What's wrong with her?" Ginny replied, "Oh, she has this condition. She just lapses into a coma sometimes. It has something to do with her nasal passages." Oddly enough, that seemed to satisfy him.

We made it home alive, and through the creative use of makeup and strategically placed hairpieces, managed to duck Mike and Tone for the rest of the summer. Yet, from time to time in the eighteen years since that incredible night, I have wondered whatever became of the dynamic duo. Well, the wondering is over because three months ago, Mike rose like a phoenix from the ashes to haunt Ginny's life again. He tracked her down through the elaborate system of contacts he'd developed over the years. (Not all of them legal, I'm sure.) Since she was still single, Mike felt certain the two of them were destined to be together. Ginny tried her best to disabuse him of that notion. She flat-out refused to 1) meet him in a public place, 2) go to his apartment, or 3) invite him to hers. She finally had to concede that she could not prevent him from driving past her building if he wanted to, this being a free country and all. "Okay, it's a start," Mike said, encouraged. (She's applying to the witness protection program even as I write this.)

"So, what on earth have they been doing all this time?" I asked Ginny when she told me about the phone call.

"Well, they found something they liked and stuck with it," she said.

"Prison?" I asked.

"No, mushrooms," she answered. "Well, actually there were some drug and prison interludes, followed by a stint in the city sewer department, but that all ended back in the late '80s. For the past seven years they've been running a successful specialty mushroom business. You know, high-end products like portobellos and shiitakes. They sell to places all over the country. They wheel, they deal. I think Tone's even traded in his Quiana for Armani."

"Unbelievable," I said.

"And get this, they call the company 'Fun Guys' Fungi,'" she snorted.

"That would be, like, a joke and that, heh-heh," I said. "Gee, I guess they're not just your average felons anymore," I added almost wistfully.

Ginny laughed and said, "Lee, I'm telling you, those guys are an enigma with a capital N."

And so they are. I guess the longer you live, the more you are shocked and amazed at the twists life takes. The older I get, the more I realize how impossible it is to predict the way things will turn out because life is just too full of surprises. Still, I think it would be a really good idea if some kind of legislation were enacted to regulate the dispensing of Polo. The stuff remains too dangerously available to suit me. There are some surprises I—and the world—could do without.

Made in the USA
Columbia, SC
05 January 2019